AF352478

The Cultural Economy
of Falun Gong in China

Studies in Rhetoric/Communication
Thomas W. Benson, Series Editor

The Cultural Economy of Falun Gong in China

❧ A RHETORICAL PERSPECTIVE ❧

Xiao Ming

THE UNIVERSITY OF SOUTH CAROLINA PRESS

Published by the University of South Carolina Press
Columbia, South Carolina 29208

www.sc.edu/uscpress

Manufactured in the United States of America

20 19 18 17 16 15 14 13 12 11   10 9 8 7 6 5 4 3 2 1

Library of Congress Cataloging-in-Publication Data
Xiao, Ming.
  The cultural economy of Falun Gong in China : a rhetorical perspective / Xiao Ming.
      p. cm. — (Studies in rhetoric/communication)
  Includes bibliographical references (p.   ) and index.
  ISBN 978-1-57003-987-4 (cloth : alk. paper)
  1. Falun Gong (Organization) 2. Religion and politics—China. 3. Communication—
Religious aspects—Falun Gong (Organization) 4. China—Religion. I. Title.
  BP605.F36X56 2011
  322'.10951—dc22

                              2010052330

This book was printed on Glatfelter Natures, a recycled paper with 30 percent postconsumer waste content.

To my family

CONTENTS

Falun Gong is a folk religion founded in the People's Republic of China in 1992 by Li Hongzhi. Falun Gong appears to have grown rapidly, provoking strong opposition from the Chinese state and the Communist Party. Li Hongzhi left China in 1995; in 1999 the government declared Falun Gong an illegal organization.

In *The Cultural Economy of Falun Gong in China: A Rhetorical Perspective*, Xiao Ming examines the rise of the Falun Gong as a rhetorical exigency. Beginning in the late 1970s, China embarked on economic reforms that have created enormous wealth but have also resulted in widespread economic suffering and social dislocation. China has created a market economy in which economic well-being is an individual responsibility, but at the same time the Chinese government has not allowed freedom in the spheres of religion, speech, politics, and culture. The increasing numbers of Chinese who are left behind by the market economy also find themselves unsupported by a social safety net and are denied the opportunity to organize for change or mutual support. With support for health care declining, many Chinese have turned to Falun Gong, attracted by its claim to be able to restore physical and spiritual health in the tradition of Chinese practitioners of *qigong*, who offer health and enlightenment. According to Xiao Ming, Falun Gong also teaches its members to discover a sense of moral purpose, liberating them from their status as victims and transforming them into agents of change. And yet, writes Xiao Ming, the Chinese government crackdown on Falun Gong appears misplaced because the movement does not claim a political agenda. Instead its threat lies in its noncompliance with the assumptions of the state: Marxist materialism, authoritarianism, and scientism.

The Cultural Economy of Falun Gong in China traces the practice of revolutionary rhetoric in the Chinese Communist Party and its development in the People's Republic, describing the rhetorical difficulties the party encountered after it embarked on a period of postsocialist, market-based economic change. This study also shows how the Falun Gong responded to the widespread sense of dislocation in a manner consistent with Chinese understandings of mind and body, intellect and spirituality, and individual and society. The figurative rhetoric of Falun Gong and its leader, Li Hongzhi, writes Xiao Ming, is well adapted to the Chinese situation. Falun Gong is especially effective in employing "indirect communication."

Xiao Ming concludes this study of the rhetoric of the Falun Gong by observing that, contrary to what might be the Western assumption, the Chinese people do not appear to be fighting for democracy, trying to develop a Western-style public sphere, or striving to become citizens of a liberal democratic society. In a study richly informed by the rhetorical scholarship of recent decades, Xiao Ming also suggests that "Anglo-American rhetorical theory" needs to question its assumptions about its own universality.

In recent years the Studies in Rhetoric/Communication series of the University of South Carolina Press has published two other books about Chinese rhetoric, Xing Lu's *Rhetoric in Ancient China* (1998) and *Rhetoric of the Chinese Cultural Revolution* (2004). Xiao Ming's *The Cultural Economy of Falun Gong in China* is a welcome addition to the series and to its developing list of works on rhetoric in China.

Thomas W. Benson

ACKNOWLEDGMENTS

This book would not have come to fruition without the wisdom and help of teachers, colleagues, and friends. I wish to express my gratitude to all who made this project a success. I first want to thank Dr. John Lyne, my former academic adviser, who continued to assist me long after I had completed my graduate studies. Dr. Cho-yun Hsu provided invaluable insights. Dr. Ronald Zboray helped me with the first chapter. Dr. Seymour Drescher's constant encouragement kept my spirits up. Dr. Lester Olson, Dr. Carole Stabile, and Dr. Gordon Mitchell offered valuable input. Dr. Barbara Warnick, chair of the Communication Department at the University of Pittsburgh, provided me with financial support to complete my manuscript.

I also wish to thank the anonymous reviewers, whose suggestions helped to improve this book, and Jim Denton at the University of South Carolina Press, who never gave up on my project. The following people also helped to make this book possible: Dr. Jonathan Sterne, Sandy Gorman, John Wills, Bradley Collignon, Emily Raine, Kaitlin Pike, Jeffrey Malecki, and Drew Mackie.

Prologue

WHAT IS FALUN GONG? Its leaders call it a folk religious group that promotes a health regimen and moral cultivation. Its supporters view it as an organization of religious dissenters that challenges the orthodoxy of the official establishment. Its ideologues say it is an inevitable product of China's transition to a market economy. Its opponents label it a grave threat to national stability and ideological unity. Finally some cynics charge that it is a cult spreading superstition.

Each of these definitions has some validity. None, however, captures the essence of Falun Gong, which lies not in the many ways its significance is configured, but rather in the nature of its dissent. It challenges the Chinese leadership's ideology concerning politics, culture, religion, science, and health care, which has long been unquestioned in contemporary China. The issues Falun Gong has raised—often not in overtly political proclamations but as alternative moral discourse encoded in theological terms—deviate so much from, and conform so little to, established views that this religious group is rightfully considered, by sympathizers and foes alike, to be a heterodoxy warranting public and scholarly attention.

To answer the question "What is Falun Gong?" we must first examine the period in which the group arose. In the early 1990s, when the decades-old Communist leadership considered itself triumphant in regulating the bodies and minds of the Chinese people, why did a heterodox religious group rise to challenge the ideological monopoly? In a broad sense, the beginnings of the Falun Gong movement parallel the transformation of Chinese society. At the heart of the officially sanctioned economic reforms that began in 1978 is the presumed conversion of the Chinese citizen into the New Economic Man.[1] At the command of the leadership, the New Economic Man is expected to be economically savvy and dexterous at meeting the challenges posed by a market economy while also maintaining allegiance to the official orthodoxy. As the leadership envisions it, the coexistence of a revolutionary Communist mentality and an economic adeptness is possible. The leadership believes that, while the revolutionary mind-set regulates the spiritual sphere, economic aptitude can improve material life. The two can be compartmentalized.

The leaders did not foresee, however, that, when their bellies are full, the masses develop aspirations. They come to believe that they are being treated unjustly by the official institutions and praxis, and this sensibility leads to the demand for just treatment. Falun Gong epitomizes this popular sentiment.

Studying Contemporary Chinese Political Rhetoric

In the era of economic reforms, the media in China is still the instrument through which the government calls for conformity and regulates the bodies and minds of Chinese citizens. As long as the government-controlled media is the sole source of information, the government is able to create a symbolic reality. Yet China has the largest number of Internet users. With the rise of the Internet, citizens have access to potentially unlimited information and have the autonomy to express their opinions in spaces where the reach of the government is limited. The duel between such opportunities for free expression and government attempts to control free speech has attracted the attention of communication scholars. Yuqoing Zhou and Patrick Moy note that, while the government attempts to control public discourse on the Internet, Internet users take advantage of the autonomy offered by the new media to bypass such regulation.[2] Zhou and Moy refer to progressive Internet users as *netizens*, noting how citizens exert their basic rights online. Zhou and Moy's critique is among the few media studies that examine the online political behavior of Internet users in China and their impact on media coverage.

Religion presents another area where the government and citizens contend for control and autonomy. In the 1980s, even though the government relaxed official policies on religious beliefs, the policy change was more nominal than substantive.[3] According to Qingjiang Yao, the Chinese government considers religious belief to be a political issue, and it has thus instructed media coverage of religion.[4] To embrace a religion other than those permitted by the government amounts to pledging allegiance to a belief other than official ideology.[5] Yao's study of the religious rhetoric of the Chinese government is significant. Though religion is a prominent issue in China, few communication scholars have examined this important topic.

The propensity of the Chinese media to be the mouthpiece of the government is the main focus of Chiung Hwang Chen's research on the coverage of Falun Gong by the government news agency.[6] As an instrument of ideology in China, the media constructs the "context" in which to view political opponents such as Falun Gong, resorting to propaganda to quench opposition. For example, during the height of official suppression of Falun Gong, a series of editorials in the *People's Daily*, the official government newspaper, disseminated the party line to Chinese citizens. Chen's contribution lies in his effort to examine the critical role of the Chinese media as an indispensible apparatus in attempts to maintain the government's authoritarian rule.

Both the government and its political opponents can use the media in unconventional ways. John Powers and Meg Y. M. Lee argue that, in addition to using media discursively, social players employ the media as a presentational aid to create symbolic conflict.[7] For example, without access to traditional mass media, Falun Gong resorts to presentational as well as discursive techniques to establish its legitimacy and to appeal to public opinion. The government also employs presentational symbolism to respond to perceived threats from Falun Gong. Powers and Lee created new approaches to critiquing the rhetorical strategies of Falun Gong, examining the presentational dimension of the media to complement their scholarly investigation.

Xing Lu and Herbert Simons's research on the political slogans from different political eras in China employs the methodology of rhetorical criticism.[8] They trace the change in political slogans from the times of Deng Xiaoping, which centered on politics, to the political slogans of the Hu Jintao era, which are pragmatic. Lu and Simons's project is an insightful analysis of how political slogans work as rhetorical strategies to aid official governance. They discuss an ideological continuity, reflecting how economic reforms continue while the leaders maintain an entrenched communist practice. As rhetorical scholars, Lu and Simons are among the first communication scholars to follow political development in China systematically and to use rhetorical criticism as a tool to critique the political rhetoric of the government in contemporary China.

Focusing on a topic on which little rhetorical study has been done, Lu has also conducted a large-scale research project on the rhetoric of the Cultural Revolution in the decades following that political campaign. The study provides important primary sources—the author's personal observations, interviews, and translations of Chinese documents. Lu synthesizes mainstream American rhetorical scholarship into her analysis of non-Western rhetorical experience. Her work should motivate future communication scholars to critique non-Western discourse and rhetorical artifacts with the help of Western methodology. Her work also challenges American scholars to reflect on the strength and scope of their methodologies in critiquing rhetorical practices other than those in the mainstream American experience.

My research continues Lu's theme in that we both draw on American methodologies to frame our critique. Yet my work also uses the lenses of sociology of religion, cultural studies, political science, sociology, and medical anthropology to examine the complexity and diversity of Falun Gong.

It is important for Chinese scholars to respond to and critique current sociopolitical occurrences in China. This book examines the rise of Falun Gong as a rhetorical exigency that attracts public and scholarly concern both in China and abroad. As my review of the literature indicates, communication scholars have conducted little major critical research on political and religious rhetoric in China. Compared to other disciplines—such as political science, sociology, and cultural studies—Chinese communication scholarship is still an underdeveloped field, both in terms of the scope of study and the employment of a variety of methodologies. To some degree my project fills this void. China is a country rich in rhetorical tradition and praxis. A systematic study of its rhetorical experience will enrich the repertory of rhetorical criticism and broaden the vision of Western communication scholars.

Rhetorical Criticism

In the field of communication, discussion continues about the role of the cultural context in rhetorical criticism. Some theorists have asserted that consideration of culture, as part of social history, is lacking in rhetorical criticism and that a reevaluation of prevailing practice is in order. Dilip Gaonkar charges that "the rhetoric critic is so occupied with the immediate pragmatics of the text that s/he has not devised an adequate strategy for signaling the constitutive presence of the larger historical/discursive formations within which a text is embedded."[9] Karlyn Kohrs Campbell suggests, "Perhaps it is time to develop courses [of public address] to teach people how to study discourse in ways that focus on assessing the role of rhetoric in shaping the course of economic, political, social, and intellectual history."[10] Gaonkar and Campbell both criticize the tendency of discourse to become divorced from cultural context—the source that provides both the constitutive framework and material of the speech. As Thomas Rosteck notes, "Public address shapes and is shaped by culture. Therefore, what is needed in our practice is a perspective that would understand both that rhetorical discourse represents the shared meanings of a particular society in history and that such discourse is itself a cultural practice that shapes history."[11]

Extending the theory advanced in Raymie McKerrow's "Critical Rhetoric,"[12] Celeste Michelle Condit explains that *critical rhetoric* draws "on its internal experiences and studies, which has consisted of a sustained critical practice to examine multiple public and social discursive phenomena."[13] Rhetoric constitutes critical practices that examine sociopolitical experiences. In Condit's view, examining the cross-cutting themes of large groups of texts places these texts within other social forces.[14] Reflecting on Condit's thesis, I argue that texts are infused with multithemed ideological import. For example, in Chinese rhetorical practices, the complexity of a text is created by the extensive use of tropes. These tropes contain an array of themes, representing both historical parables and contemporary ideographs. The audience is expected to understand these discursive devices enthymematically and respond in a culturally appropriate manner.

Condit explains how history shapes the present and how rhetoric should engage historical questions.[15] While supporting Condit's position, I argue that we should also take into consideration human intentions. Social players never make use of historical narratives verbatim. They rewrite and revise history to suit their ideological agendas. Condit also says that critical rhetoric "draws on internal experiences and studies."[16] I argue that there is a limit to how much one can draw on the internal knowledge of a discipline. As rhetorical criticism focuses on complex and multidirectional discursive practice, it is important to use the tools of other disciplines as well.

Complementary to Condit's study of discourse is the theory Maurice Charland advances in "Constitutive Rhetoric." He has developed the concept of constitutive rhetoric through the examination of how ideologues were able to call an audience, the French-speaking people of Quebec, into being as a people who then legitimated the constitution of a sovereign government.[17]

Charland emphasizes the "textuality" of audience, stressing that the constitution of audience in rhetoric is a structured articulation of signs.[18] I argue that audience indeed exists in textuality. It is subject to the dream the ideologue envisions, creating a collective public identity. Audience is thus unified linguistically, constituting a discourse community.

Charland also argues that all narratives are ideological; that is, they create the illusion of revealing a unified and unproblematic "reality," because—in giving rise to subjectivity—they obstruct the importance of discourse, culture, and history.[19] Thus one may say that narratives are the summation of long-term ideological socialization. Subjects—the audience—are the products of this political socialization. In addition an "imagined community" exists in narratives. Narrators address both an actual and an implied audience.

Charland further notes that the process by which an audience member enters a new subject position is not through persuasion, but more through a conversion in which the individual comes to identify with his or her reconfigured subject position.[20] As I see it, the function of a rhetorical process is limited and short lived. Audience members continue to step into new subject positions as they identify with the prevailing discourse. As my study indicates, subject position is not stable but responsive to a continuous procession of socialization. Thus the evolution of subjectivity is historical and extra-rhetorical. In this regard the rhetorical situation is more a snapshot capturing the audience's state of mind at particular moment than a depiction of the fluidity of an audience's subjectivity in ideological, sociopolitical, cultural, and historical transformation. To understand better the transformation of an audience's subject position, one must step away from daily occurrences and look at the larger linearity of the historical trajectory.

My research on Falun Gong affirms the American theorists' view that rhetoric shapes and is shaped by social history. I approach my topic from three angles: culture and history, discourse, and audience. Culture and history form a larger constitutive framework that impacts discourse. Throughout Chinese history those in power have been urged to learn from the classics. Classical traditions have become a primer for later generations to follow so as not to repeat historical mistakes. Repeated attempts have been made to revive the classics so that they can be used as ideological or social models. Culture and tradition frame how discourse is performed. In the contemporary era, history—whether cultural, social, or political—constitutes the frame of reference for rhetorical performers.

Culture is also shaped by discourse. In ancient China philosophers and historians wrote treatises and monographs to record and comment on previous occurrences. Though their task was to record history, the discourse was meant to be prescriptive. Future power holders were expected to modify their actions in accord with the conduct of their ancestors. In this regard discourse shapes the trajectory of how social and political history moves along. In modern times in China, politics play a central discursive role. Classical tradition and modern politics constitute a relation of form and content. Ideologues infuse historical maxims with modern content to serve political agendas.

The changing role of the Chinese audience warrants our attention. Having had no role in a closed elite political culture in the past, Chinese people are beginning to make demands on the system. They are stepping into the new subject position of citizenry to contend with the government. A new participatory political culture is forming. Moreover, in participatory politics, political communication becomes bilateral. The old political status quo, in which communication is a top-down ideological imposition, is increasingly being challenged by bottom-up communicative efforts by citizens contending for just treatment. Though the government still resorts to suppression in order to control the ideological arena, dissidents cannot be totally silenced. Resistence takes place in varying forms and degrees. Rhetoric is used as a tool to facilitate the dissident agenda.

In this study I provide background information on Falun Gong's ethical beliefs and practices, its points of contention with the Chinese leadership, its rhetorical strategies, and its reason for being. To put the rise of Falun Gong into historical context, I discuss the politics of the contemporary government, critiquing the rhetorical changes in the public address of the new Chinese leadership, represented by Hu Jintao and Wen Jiabao. I hope to give readers a better understanding of the complexity of the contemporary Chinese politics that gave rise to the Falun Gong movement.

I discuss how Falun Gong challenges the basic assumptions of Marxism, authoritarianism, and scientism—the philosophies that form the bedrock of communist political culture. I uncover the appeal of Falun Gong's treatment of the widespread somatization disorder; members see the cure as the process of unbinding a culturally linked illness. The efficacy of Falun Gong—in addition to its implicit ideological bent—lies in its leader's ability to play the role of a "cultural doctor" who offers psychosocial and affective therapy for the socially marginalized.

Falun Gong's employment of tropes encodes its potentially subversive discourse, allowing the movement to take advantage of the tropes' symbiotic relationship between form and medium and content and message. In a similar vein, the government has employed a set of ideographs to create a symbolic reality and to regulate the bodies and minds of the masses.

I also discuss Falun Gong's significance by tracing the historical trajectory of Chinese citizens' political sensibility. The last part of this study begins in the years of the Red Guards and continues through the contemporary era. Radical political changes do not occur in a vacuum, and I critique the rhetorical history of the four generations that have followed the Red Guards, tracing the torturous ways through which the Chinese people came to develop a political sensibility and providing a fuller examination of the historical context against which Falun Gong arose. By using "cultural economy" as an umbrella term, I discuss how culture relates to and functions as an organizing system of history, religion, politics, ethics, and medical anthropology that impacts the struggle of Falun Gong.

❈ ONE ❈ The Rise of Falun Gong

SINCE ITS INCEPTION in 1992, Falun Gong has attracted a large number of Chinese followers. At its height, from 1996 to April 1999, it claimed to have a membership of between 70 million and 100 million practitioners.[1] Members of Falun Gong come from all walks of life: college students, scholars, workers, merchants, and peasants. Perhaps the most interesting among these groups, however, are the roughly two hundred thousand members who also belong to the Chinese Communist Party; they range from senior party officials and eminent party leaders who once participated in the Long March to rank and filers such as party secretaries, model workers, and war heroes.[2]

These so-called Old Revolutionaries (*lao geming*), many of whom became Falun Gong spokespersons, have aroused public interest and warranted scholarly attention. Most pledged their allegiance to the Communist cause at a young age and fought for the Chinese Communist Revolution for most of their lives. Yet, when a heterodox folk religion arose, they seemingly switched their loyalty and devoted themselves to Falun Gong.

Li Hongzhi founded Falun Gong in 1992. He began to lecture and set up teaching stations in northeastern China. Similar to other practitioners of *qigong* (various Chinese systems of physical and mental training for health and self-enlightenment), Falun Gong enthusiasts initially expressed an interest in healing. Between 1992 and 1995, Li popularized Falun Gong by giving talks, publishing lectures, and selling books and other paraphernalia, building a nationwide organization. Falun Gong's main ideology focus was on freedom of speech and religion, as well as the fight for human rights.[3] At the onset Falun Gong insisted that it did not have a political agenda; its main goal was to cultivate moral elevation. However, a political overtone was apparent in the organization's actions. Observers noted similarities between Falun Gong and secret societies and millenarian sects in China's past, such as White Lotus. Earlier sect leaders denounced the corruption of the regime while espousing their own utopia as an alternative. In the case of Falun Gong, Li Hongzhi's writings are highly sectarian, as he understands himself and Falun Gong in terms of a centuries-old cultural tradition.[4] The Chinese leadership in the imperial period inevitably responded with crackdowns to maintain social order. The contemporary anticult campaign to eradicate the influence of Falun Gong resonates with this history, in which the state declared certain masters, healing forms, and spiritual practices to be false, superstitious, and evil. Boundaries were created.[5]

The government views Falun Gong differently from the way it is perceived by the organization's members. While Chinese authorities have insisted that Falun Gong is a tightly structured, well-organized, and purposeful group that is capable of achieving a variety of goals, Falun Gong has emphasized its supposedly decentralized and voluntary character. Li left China in early 1995 in response to mounting opposition within some party and government circles. Hoping to provide some sort of organizational base for Falun Gong, Li's assistants in Beijing applied for registration as a "social organization," first to the National Minority Affairs Commission, then to the Chinese Buddhist Federation, and finally to the United Front Department. All applications were denied.[6] Instead the government created even more restrictions on Falun Gong and declared it an illegal organization on July 22, 1999.

Falun Gong is one of the largest nongovernmental organizations in the history of the People's Republic of China. Economic reforms and the turn to a market economy created the space for Falun Gong to exist, but the continued political dominance of an authoritarian regime and communist ideology led to its suppression.

The introduction of economic reforms in 1978 was greeted by praise within China and from many in the West. The reforms were seen as an opportunity for China to walk away from communism and join the ranks of other modernized countries. The reforms were also perceived as stepping-stones for China to achieve Western-style liberal democracy. As with any sweeping change, however, the economic reforms brought both successes and failures. While some Chinese experienced a significant rise in their living standards, others fell through the cracks. A few Chinese theorists and academicians have come to call these marginalized individuals the "Socially Vulnerable Group" (*ruoshi qunti*). According to Zan Jiansen, a professor of political science at Shanxi University, the Socially Vulnerable Group consists of those whose income, social status, civil rights, and competitive ability are in a disadvantageous position. The group typically consists of the unemployed, the unskilled, women, and the elderly. Appearing as a result of social transformation and economic marketization, this group, some feel, has been abandoned by society.[7]

Chinese scholars studying the so-called Socially Vulnerable Group tend to divide its members into four subgroups. The first subgroup is the "new urban-impoverished group," which includes the unemployed, those who work in unprofitable state-owned enterprises, and retirees and their dependents.[8]

According to statistics issued by the Chinese National Labor and Social Protection Agency, by June 2001 there were 13,087,000 unemployed persons who had registered with the agency. After being laid off, such people usually lead lives of extreme poverty and often remain jobless for as long as twenty-eight months.[9]

The second subgroup is called the "borderline group"—urban migrant workers. With dual urban and agricultural status, this group mainly works in mining, construction, and service industries. Urban residents are reluctant to take jobs in these fields as they tend to provide meager salaries and few benefits.[10] The migrant workers usually come from the midwestern part of China, where the economy is underdeveloped and opportunities for employment are scarce.[11]

The elderly, the undereducated, and the unskilled form the third subgroup. In general, females make up 60 percent of this category.[12] They tend to be among the first to be laid off and have little opportunity to be reemployed.[13] The elderly in China, as a socially disadvantaged age group, are worthy of special mention. By 1998 people sixty-five years old and older constituted 7.4 percent of the entire Chinese population. It has been estimated that, by the mid–twenty-first century, the elderly in China will account for half the population of people sixty-five and older in all Asia—and one-fifth of the same age group in the entire world population.[14] Dependent on pensions, these people have their lives made more difficult by the lack of a state system that provides adequate benefits and assistance. An increasingly large number of senior citizens go without the daily living assistance that they need.[15]

The fourth subgroup is a recent phenomenon: college graduates who have been unsuccessful in securing employment. Because of the uncontrolled birth rate of the 1950s and 1960s, before family planning was put in place, the children of people born in the 1950s and 1960s were graduating from high school in the 1980s and 1990s at an unprecedented level, and not all graduates were able to secure employment. The government feared that these jobless youths could cause social instability. To resolve the issue, the leadership decided to expand college admissions under the assumption that rapid economic growth would create ample job opportunities for a skilled labor force. For example enrollment in tertiary education increased from 4.47 million in 2000 to 20 million in 2004.[16] According to a recent report issued by the Ministry of Education, the acceptance rate at universities and colleges in 1977 was 4.7 percent; by 2006 it had jumped to 56.8 percent.[17] Yet, when it converted the centrally planned economy to a market economy, the leadership did not improve existing institutions of higher education or overhaul the old curriculum. The outdated curriculum was not compatible with the demands of the market economy and therefore did not prepare the

growing number of college graduates for available jobs. Under such circumstances, the more quickly higher education developed, the higher the rate of
unemployment among college graduates rose.[18] It is estimated that in 2006, 2
million college graduates were not able to find employment.[19]

The Chinese leadership sees the four subgroups of the Socially Vulnerable Group as inevitable products in China's transition to a market economy
because they lack the ability to compete and succeed. It is up to them to care
for themselves, the government believes; society has no obligation to provide
support. A 1999 editorial in *People's Daily* expresses this sentiment quite
clearly: "In the modernization process, it is *inevitable* that a certain number
of people cannot survive the fierce competition" (italics added).[20] Wang Sibin,
a professor of sociology at Beijing University, uses the term "individual responsibility" to characterize the government's explanation of social rank and
economic competitiveness. The government feels that "these people have
become socially disadvantaged," Wang Sibin writes, for "personal reasons."[21]

Contrary to what the Chinese government claims, Wang Sibin and many
others believe the deprivation suffered by the Socially Vulnerage Group is
not caused by personal ineptitude, but rather by a deficient social structure.
According to Wang Sibin, the growth of this group has both biological and
social causes. The biological causes include infancy, old age, disability, and
poor health—all of which reduce one's ability to compete. Society also plays
a crucial role: if it provided them with adequate support, the biologically
weak would not become socially weak.[22] The biologically weak exist in every
society, no matter what the social system. It is the government's responsibility to provide a safety net for these people so that they do not exert substan-
tial pressure on society. Wang Sibin asserts the Chinese government has not
made it a priority to prevent the biologically weak from becoming the socially
weak. The biologically weak often have to fend for themselves.

It is plausible that the government's favoring the socially strong over the
weak is influenced by the policy that Deng Xiaoping laid down in 1985, when
he proposed the policy of letting "some Chinese become rich first."[23] The
government never formulated a policy to help those less competent to compete in a market economy and achieve economic success. A gap between the
rich and poor began to occur. China was quickly growing into a country noted
for its inequality.

Wang Cailing sees the protection of the Socially Vulnerable Group as a
matter of social justice, a necessary component of a stable social order. According to Wang Cailing, "When the gap of income level" between the rich and
the poor "exceeds the psychological endurance [of individual social mem-
bers], it instigates social disorder."[24] Echoing this sentiment, Wang Sibin con-
tends that the Socially Vulnerable Group incurs "private pain," which leads

to broad "social pain." The former term refers to the psychological and material distress of the socially vulnerable, while the latter refers to the pressure the Socially Vulnerable Group exerts on the economy, politics, social order, morality, and ethics of society at large. Members of various social ranks experience and perceive social pain differently. When private pain exists on a small and local scale, it inflicts a minuscule impact on society, and social pain is imperceptible. In such circumstances society tends to consider private pain as an individual matter. But when the Socially Vulnerable Group grows in size and the gap between the socially advantaged and the socially vulnerable widens, social pain becomes immense. When large segments of the population are in private pain, it "leads to the potential danger of long-term social disorder," the manifestation of social pain.[25]

Advocates of social responsibility, as opposed to individual responsibility, do not represent the official view of the Chinese leadership, which insists that society is not responsible for the existence of the Socially Vulnerable Group. As Wang Sibin explains, these people have become socially disadvantaged as a result of social transformation and the system of uneven distribution. Because official policy favors the strong over the weak, these people have become marginalized.[26] Wang Sibin and those who agree with him believe that the central leadership discounts the symbiotic relationship between private and social pain; social pain is the aggregate and extension of private pain. To create a stable social order, they argue, modernization, prosperity, and social harmony must be created for the common welfare of all members of society.

How do the socially disadvantaged cope? Dorothy J. Solinger interviewed laid-off workers in China in 2000. As of autumn of that year, the official "basic living allowance" for a laid-off worker in Wuhan was 280 yuan (thirty-five U.S. dollars) per month—"itself hardly enough for eking out an existence." Of the fifty laid-off workers she spoke with, hardly anyone was receiving the full amount.[27] The odds of their gaining new employment were not good either. According to John Giles, Albert Park, and Fang Cai, between 1996 and 2001, only 35 percent of the unemployed in China were employed again within twelve months.[28] These same researchers point out how the statistics differ along with degrees of market reform. For example, in cities hit less hard by restructuring, such as Shanghai and Fuzhou, about 42 percent of individuals were reemployed within twelve months. But in Shenyang, Wuhan, and Xi'an, cities where China's heavy industries were once concentrated, only 29 to 30 percent found jobs again within twelve months.[29] For all age groups, the number of men reemployed was higher than that of women. Individuals with more education were also more likely to be reemployed. For both men and women, there was a significant decline in reemployment for those over forty.[30]

Under such circumstances, members of the Socially Disadvantaged Group suffer a strong sense of deprivation and frustration. They feel anxious, despondent, pessimistic, and helpless. While they have a difficult time accepting the reality of their situation, it is even harder for them to make self-adjustments. According to a 2001 Sichuan University research report on laid-off female workers in Chengdu City in northwestern China, "being laid-off (*xiagang*) not only caused a dramatic decrease in income, but also produced in these female workers a strong sense of deprivation and loss of self-worth. It dealt them a heavy psychological blow. A series of health and mental problems began to surface: depression, anxiety, isolation, difficulty in breathing, heart disease, and hypertension."[31]

According to the same report, 65 percent of these laid-off female workers felt victimized by economic reforms; 58 percent thought the government was ineffective in helping them find a new job; 58 percent thought that the government was responsible for their reemployment; and 44 percent did not have faith in their future.[32] One may conclude that what is perceived and experienced by citizens as somatic and affective problems are, in fact, psychosocial and culturally constructed. Or, to consider another angle and relate back to Wang Sibin's theory on "private pain" and "individual responsibility," one could draw the conclusion that the cause of and a possible solution to these issues are systemic and produced by the changes in the body politic.

Aside from the socially disadvantaged, how do other, perhaps middle-class, citizens in China make adjustments to market reform? According to a report published by the Chinese-language online weekly magazine *Chinese News Digest*, the middle class feels overwhelmed by pressure. In a society where opportunities seem to abound and everyone is in a competitive mood, the Chinese feel exhausted by job responsibilities and competition. They find it difficult to achieve a balance between their jobs and their family life. It is commonly perceived that the abundance of material goods is achieved at the expense of health and psychological well-being. They feel that the progress of modernization is not matched by the availability of psychological support.[33] In April 2006 a blog surveyed 11,113 Chinese about whether they wanted to be Chinese nationals in their next lives; 64 percent said no. They claimed that the social environment was too harsh for them to lead a happy life.[34]

The Issue of Health Care

The existence of vast numbers of citizens within the Socially Vulnerable Group raises a puzzling question: what is the role of the state in providing health care for the people of China? Though health care constitutes one of the basic elements of a safety net to guarantee the welfare of citizens, the government has done little to offer them comprehensive health care. To understand the system of health care in China, one has to review its history.

Issued in 1985, the government's "Report by the Ministry of Public Health Concerning Policy Issues in Health-Care Reform" marked the beginning of health-care reform in China. A system was set up to determine the percentage of health-care costs various Chinese citizens have to bear. According to this system, "carders" (higher-ranking government ministery employees) who joined the revolution before 1949 and full professors can enjoy free medical care. The head of a department or an associate professor gets 95 percent reimbursement for health-care costs. Apart from these groups, different institutions, schools, and companies draw up their own policies on how much they will pay toward the cost of their employees' medical care.[35]

Health-care reform is an important factor to take into consideration when examining the relevance of Falun Gong. As social-service responsibilities are decentralized, medical costs are increasingly transferred to individuals. The more localized, market-oriented approach to providing social services—together with new economic inequalities—has raised concerns about barriers to health care. Medical-care costs have escalated, while many public services and safety nets have collapsed.[36]

Facing the pressure of meeting increased social demands on welfare services, the Chinese state attempted to broaden the financial bases of existing welfare institutions and introduce a multisupplier system in order to minimize government expenditures on welfare.[37] Equity has become a critical issue in China's health-care system. Access to health care is primarily based on employment and the place of residence. In the urban health-care sector, five vulnerable groups exist: employees of unprofitable enterprises; unemployed, or *xiagang* workers; retired workers living on pensions; the handicapped; and migrant workers.[38]

Health care is a basic human need. It is also a symbol of social justice. In China, health care, housing, and employment are the three indicators of social and economic success. They are also the hallmarks that divide the "haves" from the "have-nots." The government sees the inequality as inevitable in the market economy and has not made adequate efforts to correct the problem.

It is under such conditions that Falun Gong arose. Falun Gong's initial claim to "heal" and restore health attracted immense popular support. Falun Gong member Wang Youqun, in his "Ten-Thousand-Character Open Letter to Jiang Zemin," expresses the sentiments of many people who joined the group: "I began to practice Falun Gong in 1995. Within a few days, Master Li [Hongzhi] helped me purify my body thoroughly. For the past four years,

I did not spend one single cent on medical expenses. Hundreds of thousands of people, after believing in Falun Gong, have stopped using doctors and medicine."[39]

Testimony and empirical data provide evidence that Falun Gong offers healing to the common Chinese and helps them relieve stress. Indeed most Falun Gong members cite "health reasons" as the primary factor for joining the group. The claim that Falun Gong restores health is evident in almost all the testimonies of Falun Gong members. Quantitative surveys also find that health benefits are a central reason for becoming a member of Falun Gong. For example a survey conducted by the Psychological Research Institute of the Chinese Academy of Science showed that 43 percent of Falun Gong members list "strengthening health and being rid of sickness" as the main reason for them to join the group.[40]

Falun Gong also promises to lend support to the socially disadvantaged. According to the report mentioned above, "the majority of Falun Gong members are 'the middle-aged, the elderly, women, the sick and the socially marginalized.'"[41] As Lisa Weaver, a CNN news producer-correspondent in Beijing, reported in 2000, Falun Gong was most popular in northeast China, where Chinese heavy industry was once concentrated but had recently been shut down. As a result, large numbers of Chinese blue-collar workers were laid off in this region.[42]

While the socially disadvantaged may find solace in Falun Gong, they are not the only ones attracted to the group. According to a report issued by the Sichuan Provincial Academy of Science, Falun Gong members can be divided into three main groups. The first, called the "typical" group (*putongxing*), are the core members of the sect: the middle-aged, the elderly, women, the disabled, and those with "socially borderline" personalities, that is, those who cannot fit into the mainstream culture and are downtrodden. These members tend not to be well educated, are generally from the lower rungs of society, and suffer a strong sense of "loss" in the market reforms.[43]

The second group, however, consists of intellectuals of different ages. They tend to form the backbone of Falun Gong. As a group, they are well educated, knowledgeable, and possess good social skills. Their reasons for practicing Falun Gong are not utilitarian; rather they wish to cultivate "personal character" (*xiuxing*), for they hope to find a rational explanation for human life and world affairs through Falun Gong texts.[44]

"True believers" (*wanguxing*), a minority, form the third group. They tend to be well-educated and society leaders. When they join Falun Gong, they usually assume leading positions. They often make the claim that they have mastered its texts and see themselves as saviors of humanity, society, and the universe.[45]

What is the common benefit that Falun Gong members of different backgrounds find in the heterodox organization? Both Western and Chinese scholars provide several possible explanations. According to Nancy Chen, the restoration of "personal balance, self-cultivation," the relief of "somatized disorders," and the "reframing [of] the very boundaries of public and private spheres" are all things that attract people to join Falun Gong.[46] According to the Sichuan Academy of Science study, Falun Gong recruits new members in a manner similar to many sectarian sects overseas: the leader "promises" to offset the negative life experiences that members suffer in society. These promises include the restoration of health, an end to isolation, and salvation from desperation. Those who are puzzled by current affairs find answers in Falun Gong texts that explain the existence of society and humanity from a different angle.[47]

However, the reason for Falun Gong's immense popularity is more complex and profound than its immediate therapeutic effects. My research has found that Falun Gong's teachings—which are influenced by traditions from folk religions such as White Lotus, Taoism, and Buddhism—instill idealism in its members. They are taught to link their personal fates with the betterment of society at large. As a result, they develop a strong moral purpose and engage in actions that bring changes to society. They are thus liberated from the role of victims of the social system and become agents of change.

Why Is Falun Gong a Threat to the Chinese Government?

For much of the world, awareness of Falun Gong first came in 1999, when the Chinese government banned the group and arrested and imprisoned many of its members. Falun Gong practice stations were ransacked and shut down. These events were part of systematic efforts by the Chinese leadership to suppress Falun Gong. The world eventually learned that the central government had set up an office on June 10, 1999, to oversee the crackdown. The office became known as the "610 Office" in reference to its date of formation.

Beyond physical suppression, the Chinese government launched a nationwide ideological campaign to ensure that the Chinese people continued to pledge their allegiance to the central government. *People's Daily* carried daily editorials denouncing Falun Gong. Headlines for these editorials included "Cancer of the Society, Curse of the People," "Falun Gong Is Really a Cult," and "Ludicrous Heresy and Evil Intent."[48] In effect the Chinese government openly declared Falun Gong an enemy of the state.

Why is the Chinese government threatened by Falun Gong? The dissident spiritual movement does not claim to promote a political agenda to unseat the Chinese government. Its stated goal is to strengthen the minds and bodies of its followers. It is a threat, however, because—among other behaviors deemed offensive to the Chinese leadership—Falun Gong members are loyal to a spiritual leader who is a not a member of the Chinese Communist Party; they pursue an alternative ideology; and they reactivate traditional and cultural strains that are at odds with communist belief. At the core of communist ideology is intolerance for noncompliance. Thus it comes as no surprise that the Chinese government perceives Falun Gong as a threat.

Falun Gong may be especially threatening to the government because its dissent comes from subtle and complex moral, cultural, sociological, and medical anthropological roots. Falun Gong came to stand for an alternative use of the body, a somatic-turned-critical discourse, the engagement of noncompliant collective actions, and the promotion of a religious faith that challenges the basic ideological assumptions of Marxist materialism, authoritarianism, and scientism that the Chinese Communist Party supports.

Free Spaces

Falun Gong members' dissent is first found in their claims that their bodies belong to themselves, free from the interference of the state. This claim is noteworthy because it implies that an ordinary Chinese individual should have a private space of his or her own, a challenge to the government's attempts to control the mind and body. In this sense Falun Gong is advocating what social scientists in the West call "free spaces"[49]—"small-scale settings within a community or movement that are removed from the direct control of dominant groups, are voluntarily participated in, and generate the cultural challenge that precedes or accompanies political mobilization."[50] Related terms are "protected spaces," "safe spaces," "spatial preserves," "havens," "sequestered social sites," "cultural laboratories," "spheres of cultural autonomy," and "free social spaces."[51] As these terms suggest, "free spaces" carry both sociological and political connotations. They are sociological because they offer a sanctuary where the powerless can redress their grievances and find relief from the oppression of the hegemony. They are also political because the creation of such spaces provides cathartic moments when collective identities are forged and political agendas established.

The term "free spaces" is particularly relevant in Falun Gong's practice. Self-cultivation and self-nurturing of the body enable Falun Gong members to relieve their somatic pain, to engage in spiritual growth, and to empower themselves. In a sociopolitical system that emphasizes the primacy of the state and discourages attention to the welfare of the individual, such sequestered space is essential for many Falun Gong members to rejuvenate themselves so that they may deal with the harsh reality brought on by social and economic upheavals. The very action of carving out individual spaces amounts to transgressing state-sanctioned behaviors. Created to evade the repressive hand of the state, these individual spaces become "dissenting pockets" in which Falun Gong members develop an alternative consciousness with which to challenge the official orthodoxy.

In addressing the bilateral relationship between somatized discourse and the body politic, Nancy Chen discusses the role of *qigong*, the practice from which Falun Gong originates.[52] She proposes the term "breathing spaces" to refer to the literal experience of breath work and production of spaces in all possible senses—phenomenological, social, and spatial—emerged in *qigong* practices. By breathing deeply and slowly, the individual may infuse experiences of public spaces and urban sites with personal meaning and cosmological order.[53]

The term "breathing spaces" is meant to be critical of an illiberal society, as the only private space belonging to an individual in this environment is his or her breathing room. Yet such spaces, according to Chen, can become sites of resistance, as they can be both empowering and socially disruptive. Healing "practices that nurture self-cultivation," she says, "may not only promote breathing room apart from institutional time and space, but even have the potential to undo [the] official agenda."[54]

In relation to Chinese political culture, the growth of these "free spaces" or "breathing room" as pockets of resistance may appear minuscule. Yet one should not overlook their significance because they represent the efforts of Chinese people to make inroads into the once-impregnable system of communist political culture. In view of Chinese political history, it is unlikely that a bottom-up revolution will occur. Yet it is such persistent attrition that will shake the wall of political culture and force reforms to happen.

Somatic-Turned-Critical Discourse

The emphasis on the human body is important in this process. "The deployment of the body as a frame for dissent is particularly compelling in the Chinese context, in part because of the prevalence of somatization—the expression of personal and social distress in an idiom of bodily complaints and medical help seeking," Patricia Thornton argues.[55] A common theme found in the testimonies of Falun Gong members is how they fell ill and suffered bodily pains, but found hope, therapy, and consolation through Falun Gong. Although articulated as somatic complaints, these pains are nonetheless social because they link "the individual body, the social body, and body politic," as Nancy Scheper-Hughes and Margaret Lock observe.[56] In their study of individuals suffering from depression in Hunan, Joan and Arthur Kleinman discovered unusually high levels of somatized complaints associated with social stress brought on by large-scale political, economic, and institutional change.

An inordinate number of patients presented physical complaints in the absence of defined organic pathology. The complaints primarily included headaches, dizziness, and insomnia. The Kleinmans note that, in the Chinese context, "depression signifies potentially dangerous political implications: disaffiliation, alienation, and potential opposition. Here, as a complementary process to disease causation, we have the cultural construction of illness."[57] The Kleinmans point out an organic and bilateral link between the cause of the bodily pain of a citizen and the role of the body politic. While the body politic is seen as being responsible for producing the dysphoria—an emotional state of anxiety, depression, and restlessness—the patient's somatic discourse, pain without known pathological cause, can be regarded as a protest against the body politic. Adopting an approach of medical anthropology, Thornton sees Falun Gong beliefs as empowerment for its members. Falun Gong, she notes, is similar to many *qigong* practices. "Falun Gong texts" are particularly "explicit" in this regard, first presenting "a diagnosis of the Chinese body politic" that assigns moral responsibility for "somatized social ills to the party-state" and then prescribing a course of treatment that implicitly "pits the individual practitioners against the moral foundations of the regime."[58]

In this light, the private bodily pain is rarely a manifestation of pathological symptoms; rather it is psychosocial—the internalization of societal issues in human bodies. For this reason Li Hongzhi's practices attempt to direct the flow of the universe—the origin of morality—to provide a diagnosis of, and more important, a cure for, the body politic. Li demonstrates his awareness of modern politics when he urges his followers to cultivate a realigned, alternative spirituality, an act of open defiance to the official orthodoxy.

Don Handelman proposes the term "interior sociality" to describe the interrelatedness between a person and his or her social environment. As he argues, "healing does the repair and synthesis of the world, renewal of entropy, and the rearticulation of social relationship—and also does all of these analogously within the 'microcosm' of the person."[59] The somatic discourse of Falun Gong members thus becomes a form of social critique. Falun Gong members are able to reframe their somatic experience and rise above their personal circumstances to become critics of the body politic. As testimonies of Falun Gong members suggest, physical recuperation is often followed by mental reflection that connects private bodily discomfort with larger societal issues. Falun Gong members disavow their previous ideological beliefs and construct newly evolved interpretations of transforming and building an ideal Chinese society. Thus they see themselves as agents of change who are responsible for restoring a sense of ideological coherence and moral rectitude. Their actions take on moral significance.

Collective Action

Since the group's inception, Falun Gong leaders have stated that they do not have a political agenda and will never engage in activities to unseat the central government. Li Hongzhi said in "My Statement," issued on July 22, 1999, that he "would never oppose the central government at present or in the future."[60] Indeed, from the early stages of the movement, Falun Gong members have engaged in peaceful actions because they regard the government as one of their "own." For example, after the Chinese leadership declared Falun Gong a cult and banned the group's practice in 1999, Falun Gong members chose—instead of engaging in violent protests or threats—to send petitions to Chinese and world leaders expressing their bafflement and frustration and asking for Falun Gong to be recognized as an offically sanctioned religion. In an April 18, 2006, open letter to United Nations secretary general Kofi Annan, Falun Gong members said, "As law-abiding citizens, in our own beloved country, we are suddenly accused of being public enemies by a government we trust; we feel truly regretful."[61] The choice of words in this statement shows a clear attempt by Falun Gong members to make known to the world that they and their government are "one." At least in the eyes of Falun Gong members, there is no animosity between them and their government. They are only asking the government for understanding and endorsement, which they deem as reasonable requests.

However, these carefully chosen words reveal the adoption of a deliberately executed rhetorical strategy. Kevin O'Brien and Lianjiang Li propose the term "rightful resistance,"[62] which they define as a form of popular contention that operates near the boundary of authorized channels, employs the rhetoric and commitments of the powerful to curb the exercise, and "relies on mobilizing support from the wider public."[63]

Though appearing "tame" in nature—within legal boundaries—rightful resistance is nonetheless a contention that makes use of existing channels of citizen participation and relies on the consent of elite leaders. Activists work under the sufferance of and seek support from officials and journalists who can communicate their grievances to high-ranking authorities. By staying within the boundaries of legality and claiming the authorities are representatives of justice and are capable of addressing grievances, the activists attempt to create a viable environment to safeguard their rights, rather than rouse the animosity of the power holder. In an illiberal society, this type of "outflanking tactic" has worked effectively in expressing the grievances of citizens and safeguarding their interests.

Despite publicly claiming to be a law-abiding and peaceful religious group, Falun Gong is nonetheless launching collective actions of a political nature.

The group's peaceful sit-in in Zhong-Nan-Hai demonstrates this point. The action is uniquely Chinese. As Xueguang Zhou argues, "Collective action in the Chinese context manifests itself not only through open resistance and demonstration, but also in more subtle forms of non-compliant behavior that fall outside the conventional scope of collective action. In a sense, collective inaction is an invisible 'sit-in' in the Chinese political context. Its message is loud and clear, even without symbolic actions."[64]

Zhou's comments are instructive. He points out how and why these particular types of protests have worked effectively in an unfriendly environment. Messages of resistance are conveyed in a "legitimate" and yet subtly "subversive" manner. The resisters do not aim for tangible results but rather to make the symbolic actions of being heard and seen.

The increasing occurrence of collective actions suggest a Chinese mentality. Citizens look to collectivities as the locus of power, though the groups may assume new configurations. Throughout Chinese history, social members have relied on collectivities for their identity. In the new era, citizens retain the mentality that the voice of many is stronger than one. They feel as though the message they send is important, but the sheer number of group members conveys strength and determination.

Falun Gong's Critique of Authoritarianism and Scientism

Falun Gong promotes the primacy of individuality by making human interests its ultimate concern; thus it forms an antithesis to the basic ideological assumptions of the Chinese leadership, which privileges the state and collectivity. Since 1949, when the People's Republic of China was founded, the leadership has upheld an ideology of subordinating the interests of individuals to the cause of the state. In contrast Falun Gong advocates the achievement of physical health and spiritual fulfillment by individual Chinese citizens, thus foregrounding personhood.

While authoritarianism in China presupposes that Chinese people need ongoing ideological reform, Falun Gong endorses the belief that, through cultivating moral attainment, humans are capable of transforming themselves. For example, by practicing *qigong* exercises, a Falun Gong practitioner improves his or her *xinxing* (heart and nature) and achieves moral transcendence.[65] In this process the bad karma within the individual is turned into *de* (virtue).[66] Falun Gong members believe that, when citizens collectively engage in moral self-cultivation, society will become a "good society." With its promulgation of self-rectification, Falun Gong implicitly challenges basic authoritarian presuppositions.

Falun Gong also challenges the belief in scientism upheld by the Chinese leadership; this philosophy states that science is the primary cultural principle capable of solving all problems in the realm of human affairs.[67] Scientism reduces human feelings to a secondary position behind logic and reason. Principles of science and technology—the insistence on truth and objectivity over subjectivity and human feelings—are held almost sacred. Reacting to this stance, Falun Gong offers a critique of the official position by promoting an alternative value system: its professed primary concern is the welfare of the Chinese people and the endorsement of human subjectivities.

The Rhetorical Strategies of Falun Gong

The Chinese leadership suppresses Falun Gong in mainland China with the help of state machinery. As a result, the Falun Gong movement has gone underground. In 1995, after Li Hongzhi went into exile in the United States, Falun Gong moved its headquarters from mainland China to the United States and parts of western Europe. In spite of this seeming setback, Falun Gong, rather than the Chinese leadership, is winning a symbolic victory in the court of public opinion, especially on an international scale.

Falun Gong employs a series of rhetorical strategies to ensure its long-lasting influence. Its members' unwavering dedication to their cause has won them the sympathy and support of people all over the world. Ian Johnson, the Beijing correspondent for the *Wall Street Journal* who won a Pulitzer Prize in 2001 for his reporting on Falun Gong, wrote of Chen Zixiu, a Falun Gong member who had been arrested by Chinese officials: "The day before Chen Zixiu died, her captors again demanded that she renounce her faith in Falun Dafa. Barely conscious after repeated jolts from a cattle prod, the 58-year-old stubbornly shook her head. Enraged, the local officials ordered Ms. Chen to run barefoot in the snow. . . . She crawled outside, vomited and collapsed. She never regained consciousness and died on Feb. 21."[68]

Qingliu, a Falun Gong publication, reported the testimony of another arrested Falun Gong member: "Freedom of belief is the basic right of humanity. It is won with human lives. Therefore, everyone should respect this right. You and I may have different beliefs, and I respect your right to have a different belief. But if you use force to change my belief, superficially your purpose is achieved, but you cannot change my mind."[69] Many stories of how Falun Gong members would rather give up their lives than renounce their faith are distributed through all media outlets managed by Falun Gong. In these reports Falun Gong members are portrayed as heroes, not as victims. The intention of such reports is to invoke a strong sense of sympathy in the audience.

Falun Gong endeavors to seek international endorsement. Their efforts include, for example, writing open letters to world leaders such as Kofi Annan at the height of Falun Gong's suppression and to President George W. Bush on the eve of Hu Jintao's April 2006 visit to the United States. The authors are essentially saying, "We have something important to say, and we want to be heard in the most public and respectable manner possible." Falun Gong is also successful in achieving visibility. For example, when Chinese leaders visited Paris in 2004, Falun Gong members protested by wearing bright yellow coats emblazoned with large, bold characters for "Falun Gong" on the back. Their subsequent arrests were highly publicized by the international media, prompting one newspaper to use the headline "French Police Arrest American, UK, Danish, French Citizens for 'Wearing Yellow' During Chinese State Visit."[70] Though Falun Gong does not have direct lines of communication with Chinese leaders, fighting an international public-relations campaign has proved effective.

Falun Gong also aims for emblematic effects. For example, because Falun Gong is a dissident movement working against an authoritarian regime, having its members arrested by the police in a highly visible manner suggests a violation of human rights. Another example of symbolic action is the group's lawsuits against Chinese leaders in international courts.[71] The legal verdict is much less important than the process of bringing the "guilty" party to justice. For suppressed Falun Gong members, the process itself is empowering. Though the Chinese leadership may have access to "real" state power, they and Falun Gong are on equal footing in the face of international law. In the same manner, though international courts may not reach verdicts in their favor, the action of bringing the Chinese leaders to court symbolizes Falun Gong's moral superiority.

Falun Gong extends its influence through the use of the Internet. Hundreds of Web sites maintained by practitioners throughout the world and in multiple languages, promulgate a wide range of content and strategies, including online teachings of Li Hongzhi, testimonies about the benefits of Falun Gong, personal experiences of practitioners, news of government crackdowns in China, counterpropaganda against the Chinese media, online forums, and announcements of Falun Gong activities.[72] The employment of the Internet as a tool of communication enables Falun Gong to overcome geographic, material, and spatial limitations to reach the widest-possible audience.

Domestically the rhetorical strategy adopted by Falun Gong has proved effective as well. As Kevin O'Brien and Lianjiang Li note, in large-scale resistance movements in contemporary China, "the intended audience does not have to make any special effort. They can stay indoors, open their windows and listen, or simply walk outside and watch what is going on."[73] In an illiberal society, it is crucial to stay within the boundary of legality if one does not wish to be harshly rebuked or repressed. The rhetorical strategies of Falun

Gong fit what John Bowers and Donovan Ochs call "petitioning of the establishment," moves that fall within "the normal discursive or [extrarhetorical] means of persuasion,"[74] which are "non-agitational" in nature and "in order."[75]

The Politics of the Chinese Leadership

In order to understand the negative response to and subsequent suppression of Falun Gong, it is necessary to review the political mind-set of the Chinese leadership so that we understand the historical context and why the ideology of the Chinese leadership remains frozen in a bygone revolutionary period while Chinese society is moving forward. Many Chinese remember the speech President Jiang Zemin delivered on July 1, 2001, to celebrate the eightieth anniversary of the founding of the Chinese Communist Party. In his address Jiang announced that the party would henceforth allow capitalists to join. The move was considered monumental because until then, the party had regarded capitalists as enemies. Jiang's gesture was seen as a move toward liberalization, creating a party of coalition with members who were formerly political adversaries.

Jiang's action indicates that the regime's legitimacy has become a primary concern for the central leadership in the reform era. The government's attempt to safeguard its rule is reflected in its promise that China has become a "pluralistic" society where the Chinese experience considerable measures of freedom. As Jiang said in his July 1, 2001, speech: "Since the economic reforms, new changes have taken place in the formation of class structures of our country. There have appeared founders and technical personnel of non-governmental business enterprises, managerial and technical personnel employed by foreign enterprises, and private business owners. In addition, many people change jobs between different systems of ownerships, different trades and professions."[76]

Jiang's remarks point to a tremendous change in Chinese society: before the economic reforms, a Chinese person stayed in one job until he or she retired. Now they can easily switch jobs. However, the evidence of pluralization cited by Jiang reflects only one dimension of China's reform, and characteristically it is of a nonpolitical nature. Changes in the realm of politics include a weaker party-state, the appearance of many unofficial associations, and above all, the awakening of a greater political sensibility in the Chinese people, represented for example by the Falun Gong movement.[77]

These changes brought complexity and contradictions. While the Chinese leadership continues to initiate economic reforms, it resists any attempt to introduce major transformation of the communist political system. Thus the political stagnation the Chinese leadership prefers and the challenges the economic reforms pose to Chinese society have made the national modernization drive uneven and inconsistent. Many Chinese-studies scholars perceive the current conditions in China as perplexing. As Børge Bakken says, "The quest for both more and less control, both purity of behavior and freedom to choose one's behavior, characterize the emotions of today's Chinese standing on the threshold between tradition and modernity."[78] Coming from a slightly different angle, Merle Goldman and Roderick Macquhar refer to the contradictions in Chinese reforms as "a paradox of the post-Mao era."[79] There is a dichotomy between Chinese economic growth and its increasingly fragile party-state, which is expressed in both the leadership's outdated and unheeded emphasis on centralized control and an increasing social pluralism. The modernization drive in China is therefore an uneven progression. Ian Johnson explains why political reforms and economic reforms seem to have a symbiotic but incompatible relationship: "Economic reforms have progressed to the point that a true market economy is only possible by adopting political reforms—which, put simply, means some sort of an end to the Communist Party's monopoly over power. Only this step can pave the way to a real market economy, which requires a fair judicial system, less corruption and transparent regulations."[80] The Chinese leadership holds the utopian vision that economic reforms and political reforms are unrelated matters. While a market economy can put China among the world economic superpowers, it is still possible, the government believes, for the leadership to continue to regulate the ideological beliefs and practices of the Chinese population.

The official attempt to separate the spheres of political and economic reforms runs counter to the growth of political sensibility among the Chinese people. Concerning the competitive relationship between an illiberal rule and citizens' demand for democracy, it is helpful to recall the words of the nineteenth-century French political thinker Alexis de Tocqueville: "Patiently endured so long as it seemed beyond redress, a grievance comes to appear intolerable once the possibility of removing it crosses men's minds. For the mere fact that certain abuses have been remedied draws attention to the others and they now appear more galling; people may suffer less, but their sensibility is exacerbated."[81]

Referring to this statement as the "Tocqueville Paradox," Minxin Pei argues that what Tocqueville describes is a phenomenon common to authoritarian regimes that initiate limited reforms.[82] The leadership believes that, once people's physical lot is improved, they will be content and make no other demands on the system. The legitimacy of the government is thus safeguarded. Yet once the leadership alleviates some oppression, the citizenry will become more sensitive to subtle mistreatment in all forms. For example citizens will demand the right to be treated with respect or will hold government more accountable for the failings of the system. The occurrence of Falun Gong is testament to this claim.

What happens when the regime in China wants to improve people's living standards without overhauling the political superstructure? In the face of a changing and fluid reality, the official insistence on communist norms reflects the inflexibility and rigidity of the government's mind-set. Chinese-studies scholars describe this behavior as clinging to a "utopian vision." Reading from another angle, Bakken argues that when norms are not allowed to fluctuate or no longer have a basis in social practice, they turn into "super-social norms."[83] Consequently the stagnation presents a problem for the regime in its attempts to establish social standards during a period of reform. Bakken writes, "Instead of having an integrative and cohesive effect, the inflexible and 'super-social' norm becomes a challenge to order."[84]

Bakken's prediction proves to be true in present-day China. A stagnant moral order is coming into sharp conflict with society. As Karl Mannheim says, with a utopian mentality "we get a reappearance of the concrete promise of a better world. For this mentality, promises of a better world removed in time and space are like uncashable checks—their only function is to fix that point in the 'world beyond events.'"[85] Ideologues hold on to the "utopian" vision, which is removed from time and space; yet this imagined society forms the ethos for policy making and implementation.

The occurrence of Falun Gong caught the central leadership by surprise, challenging a long-held official belief that as long as it is in command of politics, the military, and the state machinery, the leadership will be in full control of the minds and bodies of the Chinese people. As Jiang perceived it, this was true during the revolutionary era, and it should remain true during the contemporary period of market reform.

In this regard the suppression of Falun Gong is an example of how the leadership still clings to the belief in the ability of coercion and state machinery to end deviant behavior among the Chinese people. At the height of the officially sanctioned anti–Falun Gong campaign in 1999, all the allegations against the movement were about control, particularly mind control. One *People's Daily* editorial stated emphatically: "[We] must fully understand the political nature of Falun Gong; [we] must realize that Falun Gong is a political force attempting to contend with our Party and government. Falun Gong is a political dissenting force that negates Marxist ideology. And Falun Gong attempts to fight with our Party for the control of the broad masses and for the control of the ideological arena."[86] This passage indicates how an illiberal regime tackles dissent. Any deviation from conformity, however unpolitical in nature, is branded a political transgression. To the Chinese leadership, citizens belong to either one camp or another, "us" or "them." There is no middle ground. In June 1999 the Chinese government formally declared Falun Gong a "cult." As a *People's Daily* editorial published that month points out, "A cult is a cancer to society. It is an international phenomenon. It cannot be tolerated by any responsible government. Organizations of cults usually assume the false pretense of religion, falsify *qigong*, distort religious scriptures, deify cult leaders, spread superstitious theories, and control the masses."[87]

In Chinese terminology, if the government brands an organization a "cult," it means the group is deviant, illegitimate, and the target of public accusations and official censorship. It becomes a public enemy of the government, the nation, and the people.

Falun Gong remained a central political issue when Hu Jintao, the Chinese leader of the fourth generation, was elected to succeed Jiang Zemin in 2002. Many observers from abroad were optimistic that he represented a new generation of leadership that was politically moderate and likely to implement bold political reforms in one form or another.[88] His subsequent actions proved these assumptions wrong. Hu appears not to have departed markedly from the party line of his predecessor. He continues to promote Jiang's sociopolitical ideology, which is called the "Three Represents,"[89] and he steadfastly defends the Communist Party's monopoly on political power.[90] For example, on New Year's Eve of 2005, Hu delivered a special message to all Chinese in China proper, Hong Kong, and Macao. Reviewing China's achievements in 2004, he said that the nation succeeded in "building a relatively prosperous society and pushing forward socialist modernization by taking Deng Xiaoping's theory and the political principles of the 'Three Represents' as its overarching ideology and implementing a scientific concept of development." He pledged to give priority to "advancing the economic reforms and opening up to the outside world" in the coming year and to make "arduous efforts to build a harmonious society and continue to push forward socialism with Chinese characteristics."[91] Political terms such as "to continue the 'Three Represents,'" "to implement a scientific concept of development," and "to push forward socialism with Chinese characteristics," all indicated that he planned to continue to follow the party line. As if to prove his determination to uphold the old political order, he said, according to an online blog, that his administration was going to "use an iron fist" (*jue bu shou ruan*) to control the public opinion.[92] He also said that China should learn from Cuba and North Korea.[93]

Hu has stuck to his beliefs, which he has demonstrated through his endorsement of restrictive policies and government actions. Under his watch, at a meeting of national governmental media organs, a new policy was put into effect that banned twenty-nine news topics, including peasants' petitions to the government, protests against dismantling and relocating citizens' residences to make room for government projects, and social unrest among the common Chinese.[94] As many who follow current events in China have observed, these issues arise as reactions to what people consider unfair treatment by the government. Banning the publication of articles on sensitive topics was a regressive turn.

Although he continues to hold to the old political line, Hu is introducing major changes in official public address. For example he has adopted new rhetorical strategies and key terms in his public speeches to safeguard the legitimacy of the regime. Recurring phrases in official address include "people are the essence" (*yiren weiben*), "heart tied to the masses" (*xin xi baixing*), and "close to people and love people" (*qinmin aimin*). At a meeting of the Chinese Communist Political Bureau on March 27, 2006, Hu said, "[We] must insist on building [our] party for public interest and to stay in power for the sake of the people."[95] In a much-publicized visit to Harvard University in May 2005, Chinese premier Wen Jiabao used the same rhetorical strategy on an American audience: "Since 1978, we have ultimately found the right path of development, that is, the path of independently building socialism with Chinese characteristics. The essence of this path of development is to mobilize all positive factors, emancipate and develop productive forces, and ensure and protect the freedom of the Chinese people to pursue happiness."[96] Wen made the topic of his speech the government's role to "protect the pursuit of happiness of the Chinese people."

Why this change in the official public discourse? What is the rationale for the new leadership to propose that the "people" have become the focus of official policy making? Why does the government continue to ban media coverage of sensitive topics and expressions of dissent? According to Wenfang Tang, the Chinese government, though still retaining its authoritarian nature, increasingly realizes the importance of public opinion in regard to its ability to control. In response the government has established channels, however limited, for the public to voice opinions and concerns. Tang notes that one can see "improvements in the mechanisms that link public opinion and government decision making," including recent developments in "implementing rural and urban local elections," the growing importance of the "legal system," the rising "public activism of the media," and increased "responsiveness of the government ombudsman system."[97] Tang lists work units, government ombudsmen (*shangfang*), officially endorsed mass organizations—such as labor unions, women's associations, youth leagues, and writers' and artists' collectives—and the media (that is, letters to the editor or calls to a television station) as channels through which citizens may express public opinion.[98]

Although they exist as outlets for expressing public concern, these channels are still, without a doubt, officially sponsored mediums. Therefore the public has limited latitude in what they can say through them. The Internet, however, has changed much of this; in recent years, an increasing number of citizens have gone to cyberspace in order to express their thoughts more freely. In 2005 China had 100 million Internet users accessing six hundred thousand Internet sites.[99] Chinese citizens can look through personal blogs, journals, and other online publications that expose alleged scandals involving the Chinese government.[100] The Internet in China is difficult for the government to monitor or control completely. To counter this problem, on January 25, 2006, the Chinese government signed an agreement with Google that created a way for the government to block sites it did not want the Chinese people to see.[101] The Google agreement is one of many attempts by the leadership to limit access to the Internet and to monitor its use.

No matter what form expression of "public opinion" assumes in China, one thing is certain: the government cannot overlook it. Indeed, according to a June 12, 2005, *People's Daily* editorial titled "[We] Must Not Provide Channels for Erroneous Ideology, and It Is Vital to Establish a Battlefield": "The ability for the ruling party to safeguard power is an important task. To strengthen state power, it is essential to ensure the leading position of Marxism. It is urgent that we establish a fortress to protect our ideology. When our enemy wants to bring disorder to [the Chinese] society, they inevitably sabotage the ideological front first."[102]

If unchecked, public opinion could challenge official orthodoxy. The Chinese leadership believes it must redirect and reshape public opinion to remain legitimate; changes in official public address reflect these attempts. An editorial titled "How to Develop Our Ability to Handle and Direct 'Public Opinion,'" published on the *People's Daily* Web site on June 12, 2005, explains the official rationale: "It is vital to administer management of mass media, direct public opinion, and influence through official ideology the increasingly diversified society and ideological trend. Only by doing so can our party safeguard its power and leading position."[103] The government has come to the conclusion that top-down administered coercion is no longer effective. The mass media (including popular culture), public opinion, and the Internet are "public spaces" over which officials should exercise control.

In a country where public discourse between the leadership and citizens has traditionally been carried out in top-down form, why does public opinion suddenly become the official focus? To answer this question, let us look at the classic definition of the term. According to Mona Ozouf, "public opinion" was initially defined as "poll opinion" or "heterogeneous opinions."[104] In prerevolutionary France in 1789, the philosopher Jacques Necker equated public opinion with a constellation of terms such as "public mind or spirit," "generalized protest or free-access road," "public conscience," or "public admiration."[105] As these terms suggest, public opinion implies diversity, freedom of conscience, and collective strength. Ozouf sums up the importance of public opinion in the contemporary era by stating that the "evocations of public opinion [are] 'tribunal.' As with the divine tribunal, all must appear before this infallible judge."[106]

Given the strength of public opinion as a rhetorical instrument, it comes as no surprise that the government has initiated changes in its public address. Tang claims the "sensitivity" of the political elite to public opinion is created for political mobilization and for manipulation.[107] A rhetorical analysis of the etiology of terms in official discourse illuminates how both "political mobilization" and "political manipulation" are achieved. For example, with the use of "People as Essence" (in policy making and decisions) as a new major ideograph in official political discourse, the leadership expects the audience to couple it with terms such as "devotion," "dedication," "politics for the populace," (*pingmin zhenzhi*), and "concern for the welfare of the people" (*guanzhu mingsheng*)—all of which create an image of a popular and just leadership for the people.

Richard Weaver provides an analysis we can apply to our understanding of the Chinese leadership's new rhetorical style. In *The Ethics of Rhetoric*, Weaver discusses how a single term can often initiate propositions by coupling with other terms: "A single term is an incipient proposition, awaiting only the necessary coupling with another term; and it cannot be denied that single names set up expectations of prepositional embodiment. This causes everyone to realize the critical nature of the process of naming. Given the name of 'patriot,' for example, we might expect to see coupled with it 'Brutus,' or 'Washington,' or 'Parnell.'"[108] This mental trick is not lost on the communist leadership. A June 12, 2005, editorial in *People's Daily* illuminates how the Chinese leadership attempts to create the "expectations of prepositional embodiment": "'People as Essence' is an essential concept for those in power. It is also a principle that must be implemented in our practical task. 'People as Essence' means everything should be done to realize the needs of the people, to promote their healthy development, and to meet their basic interest."[109] This passage provides a good example of the political rationale of the leadership. They employ a different constellation of the term "people" to enforce manipulation and mobilization.

To a certain extent, the official rhetorical strategy is effective. For example Wen Jiabao gained a popular nickname among Chinese farmers as the "premier of the populace" (*pingmin zhongli*).[110] As one farmer said, "To tell you the truth, I feel our leaders are more and more endearing to us now."[111] Many well-educated citizens share the same thoughts. For example Li Jiang, a professor of political science at Beijing University, notes: "The central leadership implements 'politics of the populace' not only to showcase an outward endearing attitude and working style, but also to lend [a] positive impact on Chinese political life. Consequently, a phenomenon has occurred—the cohesive power and identification of the entire nation and society are much solidified."[112] As these remarks suggest, the rhetorical strategy of the leadership has evoked the intended resonance among Chinese citizens.

Changes in the public address of the new generation of leaders indicate that they are becoming more attuned to public mood. With the growth of more diverse and liberalized citizenship, the leaders have to adopt new rhetorical strategies to meet the changing situation. One example that reflects this change is the use of flexible and endearing terms in public address to win popular support. It forms a stark contrast to the harsh and ritualized political language used by previous leaders. The new leaders seem to have realized that popularity has to be earned through strategy, not brought about by force.

Falun Gong's Departure
from Marxist Materialism,
Authoritarianism, and
Scientism

FALUN GONG UPHOLDS a moral code that many scholars consider a critique of hegemonic thought. The movement challenges the basic assumptions of contemporary Communist political culture: Marxist materialism, authoritarianism, and scientism, which are the ideological bedrock of the official orthodoxy.

Defined as how the masses react and articulate their attitudes toward official politics, *political culture* makes up what James Jones calls "the external object," which shapes the internal structures of personality. As such, one's mental state is an "internalization" of one's social and political environment.[1] It can be said that the Chinese government has enforced the normalization of Communist values and beliefs to such an extent that for many Chinese the officially sanctioned belief system is internalized and turns into autonomous behavior. Without such internal transformation into voluntary action, the perpetuation of the Chinese revolution would not have been possible. This chapter examines how such unquestioning allegiance to the Communist cause was formed.

A key goal of the central leadership is to mold the Chinese people into so-called revolutionaries. The construction of the New Communist Man[2] turns out to be a complex rhetorical process. Contrary to popular belief, this process is not wrought with terror and coercion; rather it is based on the leadership's ability to make good use of people's innate resources and potentials along with the situational and material potential of the locale where the revolutionary is based. The process also enforces fundamental changes in the structure, operation, and attitudes of the social politics that define the Chinese revolutionary experience. Structural and institutional reform is made possible through a deliberate and well-orchestrated political discourse that creates linguistic unity. This linguistic uniformity in turn shapes social epistemology, which is articulated and applied in the acceptance and implementation of Marxist materialism, authoritarianism (Mao Zedong Thought), and scientism. Over the last forty-five years, these core Communist values have transformed a top-down indoctrination to a bottom-up collaboration so that the revolution becomes an everlasting enterprise.

The success of the indoctrination efforts provides us with an important lesson on how the government was able to turn the "unproblematic"[3] into "true believers." The three pillars of official orthodoxy—Marxist materialism, Mao Zedong Thought, and scientism—provide a backdrop for us to understand recent occurrence of the "rhetorical turn" in which the masses have developed political sensibilities.

Marxist Materialism

The leadership promotes Marxist materialism as its fundamental political belief. As practiced by the Chinese leadership, Marxist materialism is comparable to the Leninist vision[4] and refers in this context to the philosophy that only "matter" can be proven to exist. This contrasts with such philosophies as dualism, which assumes the existence of nonphysical, mental phenomena as well. D. W. Y. Kwok provides succinct definition of materialism: "Materialism is the belief that matter constitutes the only and ultimate reality of the universe. Thought and conscience are its by-products, and there is nothing real beneath or beyond matter."[5] A believer in materialism must necessarily be opposed to idealism. Denying the primacy of subjectivity and human conscience, a materialist will not attach great importance to humanistic concerns.

The ability of the Chinese leadership to adapt this Marxist belief to indigenous conditions in China demonstrates how the government is able to adapt a foreign doctrine to its homespun revolution. Mao Zedong, the founder of the Chinese Communist Party, acknowledged in his well-known work "On Practice" that the party affirms Marxist materialism: "Marxists believe human productive activities are the basic practices that decide all other activities. Through production, humans came to know their relationship with others. In all societies of class, through different means, members of different classes form relationships of production. This is the source of the development of human knowledge."[6] This passage makes several assumptions: that the source of human knowledge comes from practice, that human subjectivity is conditioned by social activities, and that objectivity is the criterion for judging all matters. These assumptions inform the theoretical basis of the Chinese Communist Party line and are the precepts that guide all Communist praxis.

The Communist attitude toward religion is consistent with the party's privileging of Marxist materialism. A document created in 1979, during the Third Plenary Session of the Eleventh Communist Party Congress, states:

"The negative functions of religion become all the more salient as human beings enter a class society, with its exploiting classes and religious professionals. It makes the broad masses of laboring people resign themselves to mistreatment and oppression, submitting to the will of Heaven in the class struggle and their struggle with nature. Therefore, Marxism holds that religion is the opium that drugs the people's spirit."[7] This passage expresses the Marxist notion that religion is counterrevolutionary because it caters to the interests of the exploiting class. Religion serves no practical purpose; it is a tool for the exploiting class to manipulate the masses. The Communist leadership describes religion as "reactionary." Religious practice in China was prohibited in 1949 and did not become legal again until 1982. The epitome of the Communist Man is one who overcomes his selfish needs and fulfills his revolutionary obligations. Implicit in this vision of a Communist personality is the lack of emotion, sentiment, or private thought, which are considered counter to Communist values and beliefs.

Wang Meng, a renowned Chinese writer and veteran Chinese Communist Party member, is critical of the officially endorsed Communist "unselfish" man. According to him, creating the goal of becoming this imagined, utopian "superman" at the expense of human needs and desires constitutes pseudo-humanism, ignores true living people,[8] and leads to hypocrisy, an accurate description of the state of affairs in China since 1949. A split personality has become common among both the elite and rank-and-file, particularly after the Cultural Revolution, when citizens became disillusioned with Communist ideals. In public everyone assumes a persona that is altruistic, unselfish, and dedicated to the revolutionary cause; behind closed doors they reveal their true natures by engaging in self-interested behavior.

It seems only natural that humanism, which has long been suppressed in China, surfaces whenever the opportunity arises. The rise of Falun Gong and its challenge to the selfless Communist superman is one such example. Falun Gong makes its ultimate concern the well-being of its members. Its tenets, beliefs, practices, and rituals all center on the primacy of the individual. Thus the group implicitly critiques the Chinese leadership's advocacy of Marxist materialism.

Because of the irreconcilable conflict between party-endorsed Marxist materialism and Falun Gong's promotion of religious humanism, Falun Gong met with stiff opposition from the Chinese leadership. In order for us to understand how this clash plays out in discursive from, let us examine the theories of He Zuoxiu, an academician (*yuanshi*) of the Chinese Academy of Science, a steadfast champion of Marxist materialism and a staunch opponent of Falun Gong. It was his accusation against Falun Gong in a May 11, 1998,

Beijing Television interview that initiated the conflict between the religion's followers and the central government.[9]

In April 1999 He Zuoxiu wrote an article on Falun Gong for the popular journal *Qingshaonian keji bolan* (A Survey of Science and Technology for Youths) that paralleled the negative coverage the group was receiving in the officially sponsored media at the time. He first argued that the so-called paranormal capabilities attributed to veteran Falun Gong members were "falsified." He recounted several anecdotal reports of incidents in which devout Falun Gong practitioners supposedly lost their minds or committed suicide. He ended the article by writing: "In Chinese history, there used to be a famous philosopher by the name of Dai Zeng. He [once] described the moral code of Zhu Xi and Cheng Yi as 'to kill with ethics.'[10] Now, those promoters of pseudo *qigong* and special capabilities, to the degree they poison youths, are worse than those who killed with ethics [in ancient China]."[11]

He Zuoxiu's analogy insinuates that the ethical code promoted by Falun Gong harms more than it enlightens, putting a negative stamp on the group's beliefs and practices. As a movement that upholds an alternative moral code, Falun Gong, He Zuoxiu alleges, is systemically flawed. Such commentary is a classical example of how a Chinese Marxist tackles political dissent.

Critiquing this sort of political tactic, James Aune claims Marxists employ a deterministic line of thinking that reduces language of dissent and disagreement to articles of faith.[12] Instead of considering Falun Gong's beliefs and practices as a form of political discourse, Marxists reduce them to superstitions and cultlike activities. When this tactic is used, freedom is denied.

In contemporary China, Marxist rhetoric undergirds the central leadership's reaction to change and contention. In other words the leadership adheres to a highly formulized political language that is reductive and simplistic. No matter how complex post-Mao Chinese society has become, its leaders mechanically employ the same political discourse and adopt the same attitudes to diverse issues regardless of their intricacy. In this regard, the contention between the leadership and Falun Gong provides a fitting case study of how the government handles a society in flux by "harping on the same string" (*laodiao zhongtan*).

While Falun Gong started as an innocuous folk religious organization, offering healing to those displaced in the market economy, the government adopted the same policy it has always applied to any sort of "dissent" throughout the political history of China and set out to suppress Falun Gong. After the publication of He Zuoxiu's April 1999 article, Falun Gong representatives demanded an apology from the editor of the journal. When their request was denied, more than six thousand Falun Gong believers staged a sit-in in front of the journal's office. The incident ultimately led to the large-scale sit-in at Zhong-Nan-Hai on April 24, 1999.

Labeling the practice of *qigong* as witchcraft, superstition, and pseudo-science, He Zuoxiu argues, "Our current task is to promulgate dialectical materialism and atheism. We must not relax in our efforts to oppose feudal superstition and any of its variations. We must discern the link between these variations and pseudoscience. In our struggle against witchcraft, pseudo-*qigong*, and feudal superstition, the circle of science and technology is unequivocally responsible."[13]

In China any popular health regimen not endorsed by the government is often called pseudoscience, for it violates "scientific Marxism." He Zuoxiu uses terms such as "witchcraft" and "feudal superstition" as denotations for "pseudoscience." Yet Aune claims that later Marxism has not been able to differentiate between "subjective agencies and objective structures."[14] It is common practice for modern Marxists to employ qualities of external experience and structure to define internal subjectivities. Subjectivities can never be agencies to bring about external changes, but external structures, such as social institutions, can.

Another common theme found in the Communist critique of deviant spiritual practices is the claim that practitioners have ulterior motives. In an article titled "Communists Must Be Atheists," He Zuoxiu writes: "Some people with ulterior motives manufacture theism; they create a new god—even a living god—in the name of religion. They in fact distort laws and regulations in legal religious activities so as to achieve their shady motives. [What is worse], some Communist party members give up their [ideological] weapons in face of the new theism in the disguise of science."[15] Although he is repeating a party line that many Chinese are familiar with, He Zuoxiu's rationale, from a rhetorical perspective, may not be initially apparent to them. His employment of a vocabulary of division, such as "us" and "them," shows a Marxist commitment to the centrality of class as a factor in history. According to Marxist thought, race, ethnicity, gender, and religion all come second in political importance to class. Class predominates all sociopolitical activities.

A rhetorical analysis of He Zuoxiu's commentary on Falun Gong also suggests how Marxist rhetoric serves, as Aune says in *Rhetoric and Marxism*, both "as a theory of revolutionary communicative practice and as a practical handbook for the management of discourse."[16] Discourse produces formulized language, creates a linguistic unity, and ultimately constitutes what David Apter and Tony Saich call "discourse community."[17] Discourse community is essential to the Chinese revolution. It binds revolutionaries together; once a commitment is made to the organization, "no matter how personalized the leadership, it claims a higher truth and demands devotion."[18]

He Zuoxiu's comments on Falun Gong showcase "the conceptual vocabulary" of Marxism, which is based on the premise that "human nature is unable to learn from its mistakes."[19] The party, a symbol of higher truth, is therefore legitimized to reform citizens. In contemporary Chinese political history, the leadership applies the same systematic thinking across rhetorical situations regardless of changing circumstances or what form dissent assumes.

Mao Zedong: The Creator of Chinese Authoritarianism

Scholars are still intrigued by the Chinese Communist Party's victory over its political opponent, the Guomingtang, the Communists' subsequent establishment of political power in 1949, and their continued maintenance of authoritarian governance. These accomplishments owe much to the Chinese leadership's savvy use of rhetoric to turn the Chinese people into true believers. Their rhetorical strategy has led to the total mobilization and active participation of the populace in social change and an establishment of control that penetrates the roots of Chinese culture.

The late Tang Tsou used the term "political integration" to describe the synchronization of beliefs and attitudes between the elite and the masses. For Tsou political integration consisted of two components: a process of disintegration in which old social, economic, and psychological commitments are broken and a process of social integration in which new patterns of socialization and behavior are made possible.[20] The Yenan Rectification Campaign of the 1940s is a classic example of the execution of these two processes. It constituted a massive attempt by the Chinese leadership to forge a new social order by shaping and reforming citizens who in turn reorder their previous ideological experiences and learn to worship new images, behave in new ways, and relate to one another in the context of a new political culture.

Yenan, a city in the Shaanxi province that served as the political base for the Chinese Communist Party between 1937 and 1947, represents the embryonic stage from which an authoritarian society later grew. The Yenan Rectification Campaign marked the beginning of a movement by the Chinese Communist Party leadership, led by Mao Zedong, to eliminate dissidents and indoctrinate new party members. Through a review of this campaign, it is possible to identify some of the essential rhetorical strategies Chinese Communist senior leaders employed in subsequent years to enlist the energies, loyalties, and skills of the New Communist Man. This is an essential discursive maneuver to unravel, for the transformation of a Chinese person into a revolutionary is at the heart of the Chinese revolution.

An investigation of how compliance is forged under the Communist leadership reveals the mechanisms through which many Communist Party members come to perform revolutionary deeds of their own accord—once they have been inculcated with the proper political values and habits. The authoritarian practices of the Chinese leadership stands in sharp contrast to the teachings of the Falun Gong movement. While the Communist leadership cultivates a total commitment to its cause, Falun Gong encourages self-development and reflection in its believers.

In 1942 the Chinese Communist Party was becoming an increasingly important force in the national political arena. The Guomingtang was rapidly losing its popularity among the Chinese people because of its corruption, impotent rule, and reluctance to fight Japanese invaders. Many people came to see the Communist Party as the only hope for national salvation, and the party therefore experienced a period of vast expansion in its membership. Of the party's eight hundred thousand members at that time, 90 percent had been recruited within the year.[21]

These new recruits posed problems for the central committee of the Chinese Communist Party. The majority of new party members were "petty bourgeoisie, young intellectuals." Of the new party members in the Central Research Institute in Yenan, 79 percent were twenty to thirty years old, and 82 percent were urban "intellectuals."[22] These newcomers brought to the party not only their hope and enthusiasm but also their own theories and beliefs as to how the revolution should be carried out. The Yenan campaign was launched in part to "ensure the commitment and adequate indoctrination" of these new party members.[23]

At Yenan the drive to achieve political integration lasted from 1942 to 1945, the earliest major political campaign in the history of the Chinese Communist Party. Over its course, rank-and-file party members were made to study important early speeches given by Mao Zedong and other high-ranking leaders such as Liu Shaoqi and then to engage in confession and self-criticism. The success of the campaign secured Mao's leadership, and the political discourse of the Chinese Communist Party formally took on an authoritarian nature.

Yenan was thus the greenhouse for the authoritarian behavior of the Chinese leadership. David E. Apter and Tony Saich aptly call Yenan the "moral moment" in the history of Chinese communism.[24] The term "moral moment" has physical, spiritual, and political implications. In the physical and the spiritual sense, life in Yenan was primitive and spartan. Yet for Yenanites this rustic setting enhanced the loftiness of their revolutionary goal. Yenan became ground zero for a movement that sought nothing less than the creation of a new world far from the center of civilization.[25] Here the party rank-and-filers developed the fervor to fight for the Chinese revolution, and the central leadership developed the blueprints for a new Communist society. The mundane world was linked to grand visions that were global, abstract, and lasting. To many Chinese at the time, Yenan had the sacred quality of a New Jerusalem.

The implementation—and, to a large degree, the success—of the Yenan Rectification Campaign relied on revolutionary discourse. This discourse was meant as a source of allegiance for party members, who learned to link their precarious personal experiences to a centralized goal; they would thereafter speak the language of revolution. In this process any vestige of individualism was to be eliminated. As Apter and Saich point out, "The goal was to create a seamless web of discourse out of which a community would be created according to the rules of collective individualism, a community in which self-enlightenment and knowledge would enhance each individual's sense of well-being and enable each person to believe that his or her own person was enhanced by the collectivity."[26]

Apter and Saich explicate the efficacy of the Chinese leadership's political discourse. Particularly important in this rhetorical strategy are the ideas of "self-enlightenment" and of an individual being "enhanced by the collectivity." The exercise of coercion is subtle and nuanced yet highly effective, for it is able to transform top-down imposition into a process of self-enlightenment and enhancement for the lower ranks of party members. Thus what is essentially coercive is made to seem spontaneous and autonomous.

Another major reason for undertaking the Yenan Rectification Campaign was to consolidate Mao Zedong's leadership within the party[27] and to rid it of dissent. In 1942 Yenan launched a large-scale review of its cadres (*ganbu shencha*).[28] The Yenan Rectification Campaign is thus also called "The Rescue Movement to Save the Fallen" (*qiangjiu shizuzhe*). According to Li Rui, who was appointed head of the propaganda section of the Central Youth Working Committee in Yenan, a campaign of "confession and report" (*tanbai jianju*) was launched to purge dissent.[29] Li was imprisoned after being wrongly accused by a colleague.[30]

Two speeches by Mao marked the beginning of the campaign. "Rectify the Party's Style of Work" and "Oppose Stereotyped Party Writing" laid out its guidelines and agenda. Mao announced that the goal of the campaign was to eliminate "subjectivism" and "sectarianism," two errors that he accused the Comintern representatives and the new party members of committing: "Subjectivism, sectarianism, and stereotyped party writing—all three are anti-Marxist. They are a reflection of petty bourgeois ideology in our party. China is a country with a very large petty bourgeoisie. A great number of our party members come from this class, and when they join the party, they inevitably drag in with them a petty-bourgeois tail."[31] The key term in this passage is "petty bourgeoisie," and its connotation is "anti-Marxist."

Since its founding in 1921, the Chinese Communist Party had proclaimed itself to be a proletarian party that served the common people. According to Mao, the "proletariat" is composed of workers, peasants, soldiers, and urban petty bourgeoisie, including intellectuals. Each of these groups occupies a different rung in the revolutionary hierarchy. The workers are the leading class of the revolution; the peasants are their most dependable allies. The urban petty bourgeoisie and intellectuals are allies of the revolution, capable of long-term cooperation with the Chinese Communist Party.[32]

However, since the Yenan campaign, the term "petty bourgeoisie" has been used by the Communist Party to refer only to intellectuals, and the term took on a derogatory tone. In the political communications of the party, "petty bourgeoisie" refers to those who—though members of the revolutionary class and allies in the party's united front against the enemy—are politically erratic and can never be thoroughly revolutionary because of their class origin.

This negative portrayal of intellectuals has a great deal to do with the general characteristics of the Chinese intelligentsia. Because of the relatively low education level of the most of the Chinese population, intellectuals constitute a distinct social class. Although few in number, they have played a vital political and social role throughout Chinese history. Jerome Grieder argues in his discussions of Chinese intellectuals that the group is a "conspicuous minority who was sufficiently perceptive and pensive to be aware of the push and change and the tug of tradition, and sufficiently well-educated and self-confident to hold and express opinions about the circumstances in which it found itself."[33] From the time of the first emperor, Qin Shi Huang (reigned 246–21 B.C.E.), the ruling class had been particularly sensitive to the outspokenness of the scholars. During his lifetime the emperor carried out the infamous Fengshu Kengru, a campaign of burning books and burying scholars in order to squelch dissent and ensure the smooth operation of his totalitarian rule.

The Chinese Communist Party inherited the cultural legacy of rulers' hostility toward intellectuals. Thus Chinese intellectuals often articulate their political sensibility at the expense of their personal safety or even their lives. In *The Gate of Heavenly Peace*, Jonathan Spence comments that, although "the cultured voices of these Chinese may seem at times too piercing, and gestures too ritualized, they still possess the essential power of leaving the apparently allotted space and marching to the center of the stage. It is often true that those who do this die earlier than the others—'before their times,' to use a simple phrase."[34]

When Chinese intellectuals joined the ranks of the Chinese Communist Party, they remained politically outspoken, thus posing a danger to the party's authoritarian rule. Mao Zedong used the Yenan campaign to stage a political showdown. He made it clear through his speeches that "petty-bourgeoisie intellectuals," unless ideologically transformed, would always be untrustworthy and occupy the bottom rung of the revolutionary ranks. This negative attitude toward intellectuals continued in post-1949 China and had devastating consequences for Chinese society.

Mao's characterization of these new party members as "petty bourgeoisie" was meant to destroy any feeling of self-importance that they might have about themselves as revolutionary participants. They were made to feel inadequate and self-doubting. Indeed, in "How to Be a Good Communist," a required text on political etiquette for new Communist Party members, Liu Shaoqi says: "We should see ourselves as in need of change and capable of being changed. We should not look upon ourselves as immutable, perfect and sacrosanct, as persons who need not and cannot be changed. Unless we do so, we cannot make progress, fulfill the task of changing society."[35] Liu's remarks help us understand Mao's criticism of new party members, providing the "legitimate reason" for the new members' self-transformation. This change has multiple implications. It means remolding and purification, and, for new party members, it is a demand to purge the soul.

This rhetorical vilification of the new party members is powerful. To intellectuals who had put their lives in danger by coming to Yenan to fight the Chinese Revolution, it was a harsh rebuke to be told that they must change themselves in order to become fully revolutionary. As they were "true revolutionaries" in their own belief, they naturally had a yearning to become the "pure" Communists demanded by the party. In rhetorical terms the call for a "pure" Communist becomes a "rhetorical vision" or symbolic reality. It is a linguistic phenomenon introduced into political discourse. The ideologue dangles a dramatic vision of the "good Communist" before party recruits, who are eager to participate in the dramatic vision and become "pure" Communists. Thus the stage is set for the subsequent process of remolding new party members.

Of course where there are villains, there will be heroes. Who, then, did the party portray as heroes? According to Mao, "compared with the workers and peasants, the untransformed intellectuals were not clean. The workers and peasants were the cleanest people, and even though their hands were soiled and their feet smeared with cow dung."[36] Regarded by their leaders as true and dependable revolutionaries, workers and peasants, the "proletariat," constitute what Richard Fagen calls the "first generation" of the revolution.[37] Even though they are not well-versed in Marxist theory, workers and peasants are the direct beneficiaries of the revolution and thus possess an abundance of raw political enthusiasm. For the Chinese leadership, the peasants and workers' lack of knowledge is a political advantage, as these groups are the least politically outspoken and the easiest to manipulate.

As the "true revolutionaries," workers and peasants became heroes or, to be more precise, role models. The Chinese leadership's call for intellectuals to follow in the footsteps of workers and peasants created a psychodramatic fantasy world. The camps of the enemy and of the revolutionary insiders were clearly defined. New party members, considered middle-of-the-roaders by the leadership, had to choose a side. As can be expected, most new party members were eager to join the camp of revolutionaries. The process of eliminating the last vestiges of individualism was complete.

Chinese leaders elicited an emotional response from new members by calling their loyalty into question and suggesting their individualism alone could shatter a harmonious group. Mao pointed out the political danger new party members, the so-called sectarians, posed to the party line: "Sectarianism within the party leads to the formation of cliques and hinders conformity and inner party unity. Sectarianism in external party relations results in centrifugalness and prevents the party from unifying the people. We must build a centralized, unified party, make a clean sweep of all unprincipled factional struggles."[38]

The authoritarian tone of this passage is apparent, captured in the key phrases "formation of cliques," "hinders . . . inner party unity," and "factional struggles." The goal of such rhetoric is to make a strong emotional impact. Mao intended to create terror by labeling the new party members so negatively that the recruits understood they, unless they submitted to being transformed and disciplined, were the enemies of the party. Mao was successful in controlling the subconscious of new party members and preparing them for the subsequent imposition of Communist principles.

It comes as no surprise that the Communist central leadership tells new party members what constitutes acceptable political behavior. According to Liu, "At all times and on all questions, a party member should give first consideration to the interests of the party as a whole, and put them in the forefront and place personal matters and interests second. Unhesitating readiness to sacrifice personal interests and even one's life for the party and the proletariat—this is one expression of what we usually describe as 'party spirit.'"[39] To be a Communist means to subjugate the self completely to the will of the party. Members must develop the "party spirit," meaning that they should be ready to die for the Communist cause. Liu eliminates the inner tension between these new impulses and old impulses that a new party member has accumulated through the socialization process. To be a revolutionary is to obey. Or, to use the terminology of Apter and Saich, the Yenan experience was a "suturing process similar to being born again."[40]

This inculcation represents the "coming into being" of the rhetorical vision of the "people." Michael McGee describes this stage as the heart of the "collectivization process," where there is a staging of the "political myth," which creates "a vision of man dangled before persons in the stage of their metamorphosis into a 'people.'" This stage is essential because "it gives specific meaning to a society's ideological commits, and it is the inventional source for arguments of ratification among those seduced by it."[41] What the leadership cultivates in new party members is a sense of *wanting* to be transformed into true revolutionaries. The formation of a "New Communist Man" became central to revolutionary rhetoric and action programs, eventually constituting the operational mainspring of the revolution.

The effectiveness of the official rhetoric is confirmed by testimonies of party members who participated in the rectification campaign. Those who came from nonproletarian backgrounds and who had recently joined the party felt that the campaign was a transformative experience. For example one party recruit who came from an intellectual background summarized her experience of the campaign by saying that it was a means for her to resolve the tension between her class background and the appropriate way to connect to the Chinese people. Once she had made this connection, she said, she was able to understand how Marxism-Leninism, as a body of universal truths and methods, would show how the Chinese revolution could be realized. The idea of communism as the final stage in an evolution presented a symbol she could fill herself because it was intrinsically empty. She could convert all her yearning into a powerful unity of self and community, China and world. Yenan enabled her to arrive at what might be called a "symbolic infinitude."[42] Here we see the formation of a new modal personality that experiences the past through the present and looks with these into the idealized future.

Several messages are revealed through this new party transformed member's comments about her "new" inner world. She apparently discarded her class origins and was willing to emulate the Chinese people. In addition she acknowledged Marxism and Leninism, or at least the Chinese Communist Party's version of them, as universal truths. Finally she saw herself as unified with the party and the Communist cause, both emotionally and rationally. Here the conversion was complete. Symbolically a "good" Communist becomes an objectified reality. From her "success" story, we get a better understanding of how the "moral capital" of Chinese revolutionaries is constituted. The conversion of this Yenanite was not an isolated incident. Many of them look back on this period with fondness. Most were young when they went there. Most received their most formative education in the context of a revolutionary simulacrum. They shared a preoccupation with virtue that would bring joy to the heart of the most devout Puritans.[43]

The Yenan campaign was a political victory for Mao Zedong as well. He not only succeeded in securing his leadership of the party but also established his political style of autocratic rule. Unconscious acceptance of the official political culture became pervasive among all strata of the Yenanites. The Yenan experience proved to be a successful learning process for new party members, The Communist leadership succeeded in creating a new political culture in which peasants, workers, and intellectual recruits alike willingly and unquestioningly embraced Communist ideology. In this regard the rhetorical strategies of the Yenan Rectification Campaign were instrumental in shaping both the motive and the motor of the revolutionary effort. At the same time, the Communist cultural fabric was woven. In 1943 the term "Mao Zedong Thought" was put forward for the first time; the expression remained a key term in the political discourse of the Chinese Communist Party.[44]

Through the Yenan campaign, Mao secured his position within the Chinese Communist Party. Moreover he further developed his authoritarian political style, which extended to the Cultural Revolution. According to Li Rui, "Using politics as the commanding ideology, and prioritizing class struggles are something Mao is a master of."[45] Since the Yenan Rectification Campaign, the term "Mao Zedong Thought" has become metonymic of the progress of the Chinese leadership in turning the Chinese people into a nation of political zealots. At Yenan the official acceptance of Mao Zedong Thought in the revolutionary discourse synecdochically signified the allegiance of the entire party to Mao Zedong's ideology. In later periods, especially during the Cultural Revolution, the term took on the connotations of "beacon," "compass," "telescope," and "touchstone," elevating Mao to the pedestal of a god. In terms of political communication, it became a catalyst for action between the party and the people. The party has used the term to rally the people and incite them to engage in further extreme political activities, and the people use it to demonstrate their political loyalty and identification with the party. In this sense the Yenan experience planted the seed for China's eventual evolution into an authoritarian society.

Hu Sheng, a prominent Chinese Marxian theoretician, summarizes the Yenan Rectification Campaign as follows: "The whole party, particularly the senior party leaders, has achieved ideological unity in their viewpoints regarding fundamental issues of Chinese revolution on the basis of Marxism-Leninism. To win the victory of the Chinese revolution, the party must follow Mao Zedong Thought as the political guideline, which combines Marxism-Leninism with Chinese revolutionary practice."[46] Hu's comments encapsulate the main results of the Yenan Rectification Campaign. An ideological unity was achieved among party members, and Marxism, or Mao's version of it, became localized. In later years, in the historical account he wrote about this period, Hu depicted how ranking leaders of the Communist Party at Yenan achieved a unified understanding of the party's policies.[47] Any dissent was eliminated, and the leadership gained unreserved support from its senior members.

In view of the effectiveness of the Yenan campaign, the Communist Party has established several rhetorical strategies to achieve its ideological agenda. Membership in the collectivity is promulgated as the criterion for a true revolutionary. Yet this goal is not imposed. Rather a new party member is made to feel enhanced by the collectivity. In other words the party places emphasis on how a new party member derives his or her personal identity from the collectivity; individual behavior is channeled into a central goal.

"Revolutionary" language plays a central role. This language is prescriptive, providing a "grammar" for what is politically acceptable and what is unacceptable. Ideographs are created and used to augment the central line of the campaign. Ideologues act like teachers. They guide political enthusiasts through the transformation process and turn them into the true Communists the party envisions. In this regard Liu Shaoqi's "How to Be a Good Communist" is instrumental in transforming new party members into true believers. An interrelationship exists between language and social influence.

With the help of rhetorical strategies, the Yenan campaign turned into a process of self-enlightenment for new party members. The party created a learning curve for the newcomers: self-doubt, purification, acceptance, and allegiance. From then on, to be a revolutionary is self starting. Rhetorically the campaign is successful because revolution is held as a lofty goal for those eager to become "the elect." The self-enlightenment has created genuine revolutionaries, whose loyalty becomes the moral reserve for the Chinese revolution.

Authoritarianism and Scientism

In contemporary China, the party leadership has donned the mantle of scientism in its modernization drive as a complementary principle to authoritarianism and materialism. Since 1978 China has made a concerted effort to modernize its manufacturing, agriculture, defense, and science and technology sectors. The Chinese leadership touts this campaign as "the new revolutionary force to push the Chinese society forward."[48] Commenting on the Chinese leadership's perception of the sociopolitical role science and technology should play in the modernization drive, Chinese political scientist Su Shaozhi wrote: "In the tide of change in the present world, the qualitative change of the social productive forces—a new scientific and technological revolution—is the basis of the entire transformation. Without a doubt, the new technological revolution will certainly exert a deep and extensive influence on society, economy, politics and culture."[49] The scientism of this passage is apparent. Science and technology are perceived as useful not only in making modernization possible but also in affecting changes in the superstructure.

It is clear that the Chinese leadership has given science an epistemological quality. Giving science authority over the realm of human affairs is termed "scientism." D. W. Y. Kwok explains that "scientism" is applied to situations in which "the limiting principles of science have become the cultural assumptions and axioms of that culture"; furthermore scientism "deems all aspects of this order, be they biological, social, physical, or psychological, to be knowable only by the methods of science."[50]

Science thus takes on what Kwok terms "a doctrinal finality," an improbable certainty for any essential human situation.[51] Tom Sorell offers another definition of "scientism," which sheds additional light on the so-called doctrinal nature of this ideology: "Scientism is the belief that science, especially natural sciences, is the most valuable part of human learning—the most valuable part because it is the most authoritative, or serious, or beneficial."[52]

The "doctrinal" nature of scientism suggests that there is a connection among it, Marxism, and authoritarianism, as both Marxism and scientism, as ideologies, are deemed authoritative and beyond doubt. As Charles Taylor argues, practitioners of scientism "take on the role of interpreters of truth" and consequently "represent the authenticated social epistemic."[53] Science, with its "doctrinal" qualities, becomes an instrument of ideologies.

A rhetorical critique of the symbolic attributes that humans give science provides another angle from which to examine how scientism receives its potency. In his influential essay "The Ultimate Terms," Richard Weaver considers science a "God" term, for it is frequently organically linked with "fact" and, more important, "truth." Weaver explains the positive relationships between science, fact, and truth: "Quite simply, fact came to be the touchstone after the truth of speculative inquiry had been replaced by the truth of empirical investigation. Today, when the average citizen says 'It is a fact,' he means that he has the kind of knowledge to which all other knowledge must defer. The 'facts' of his case carry with them this aura of scientific irrefutability."[54] When science takes on the connotation of absolute objectivity, it establishes a positive relationship with terms such as "fact" or "truth." The discursive construction of science also reveals, in each citation of a scientific "fact," that the speaker has a stake in retaining the credibility and infallibility with his or her audience.

The symbolic properties of "science" were not lost on the Chinese leadership during the era of market reform. Throughout this period and until the present day, science and technology were perceived as the driving forces to reform the political superstructure and push the national modernization campaign forward. In the new era the Chinese leadership has sought new instruments to aid its governance and safeguard its legitimacy. Scientism clearly helps accomplish this goal.

The promotion of scientism, however, contributes to the denial of humane concerns and individuality. According to Murray Rothbard, "The key to scientism is its denial of the existence of individual consciousness and will." It creates "a fictional collective whole as 'society.'" It "attributes consciousness and will, to some collective organic whole of which the individual is merely a determined cell."[55] Applying organic analogies emphasizes the indispensable role of collectivity at the expense of the individual. Since its founding in 1921, the Chinese Communist Party has insisted on its belief in Marxist materialism. The party's denial of individuality and human subjectivity has helped to consolidate its authoritarian rule. Now scientism, with its emphasis on objectivity over human subjectivity, is seen as complementary to communism and can be regarded as a variety of authoritarianism.

The Chinese leadership's scientism has particular significance in contemporary China. While the leadership seeks to maintain the preeminence of collectivity, activists push for individuality. At this juncture the emergence of a folk religion such as the Falun Gong movement can be interpreted as an assertion of the primacy of humanity and an endeavor to challenge the pervasive scientism promoted by the leadership.

Scientism is frequently used in the government's public discourse—a practice extending back to the beginning of the economic reforms in 1978, when the leadership adopted policies favorable to developing science and technology. The first signs of this policy shift appeared in a speech given by Deng Xiaoping at the National Science and Technology Conference on March 18, 1978. In his speech Deng pointed out the role that science and technology would play in the nation's modernization drive: "In the twentieth century, it is the historical task of the people of our country to realize the modernization of agriculture, industry, national defense, and science and technology. If we do not carry out modernization, if we do not raise the level of science and technology, the power of our country won't be strengthened; the security of our country will not be protected."[56] Deng's speech laid the foundation for the leadership's science policy. A careful reading of the speech, however, reveals that Deng attributed to science a quality of omnipotence; essentially he announced that while science will make modernization possible, it will also provide a solution to all problems in the political realm.

Deng's endorsement of scientism was echoed by his successor, Jiang Zemin. On May 26, 1995, Jiang gave a speech at the Chinese National Science and Technology Conference to emphasize the continuation of science policies by the Chinese leadership. During the speech Jiang said, "It is a far-reaching and monumental revolution to insist on science and technology as the primary productive force, and to move economic construction on the track of relying on scientific progress and improving the quality of the labor force. If we do so, we not only raise productive force, but also initiate fundamental changes in production and superstructure."[57]

While Jiang's speech continued the policies drawn up by Deng Xiaoping, it also indicated a few changes. Jiang dramatically toned down the emphasis on the link between communist ideology and science, focusing instead on more pragmatic considerations. This new emphasis may point to the technocratic background of the third generation of the Chinese leadership, which includes Jiang. Jiang also suggested that the promotion of science could stimulate change in the superstructure. In other words his stance on science presupposed that science can solve problems in the social world.

How then does the leadership practice scientism? First and foremost, it uses science to aid its governance. An insistence on upholding Marxist materialism is a prominent feature of the official ideology, and the party sees science as complementary to its belief in Marxist materialism. For example, in its denunciation of Falun Gong, the leadership articulated a positive and complementary relationship between Marxist materialism and science. One *People's Daily* editorial states: "The political belief of our Communist party is science. It is truth uncovered by Marxist dialectical materialism and historical materialism. It reflects synecdochically the basic interest of the Chinese people. Therefore, we must insist on a strict administration of our party, insist on the scientific world-view of Marxism, insist on materialism and atheism, and oppose idealism and theism."[58]

To the Chinese leadership, science is capable of fulfilling the need for human spirituality, a position that has led to the denunciation of the Falun Gong movement. The Chinese leadership has denounced Falun Gong as "pseudoscience," "feudal dross," and a "fake religion" instead of seeing the movement as a beneficial institution capable of fulfilling the need for human spirituality. To counter Falun Gong, the Chinese leadership calls for the continued "education of Marxist materialism and atheism" and "the education of scientific knowledge and scientific spirit."[59] This attitude reflects a mentality that Kwok describes as "stressing science's role as a cultural system and as a model for general social values."[60] To the Chinese leadership, science will not only develop the Chinese economy, but it is also able to address human spiritual needs. Thus the Chinese leadership fuses two very different aspects of human existence, idealism and reality, into one generalized concept.

Since 1978, when Deng Xiaoping assumed leadership of the Chinese Communist Party, the party has deployed a set of new strategies of persuasion in order to maintain legitimacy in the post-Mao era. The demonstration of superior moral character exemplifies one such attempt. The Chinese leadership's identification with science helps it to be perceived by the public as having superior moral character, for the image of the scientific character created by Communist leaders is inherently virtuous. As John Brooke points out, a scientific prophet has the qualities of "seriousness of purpose, dedication, the absence of self-interest, unswerving allegiance to truth, fortitude, conscientiousness, and even righteousness."[61] These qualities may belong to a "professional" practitioner of science, but they are also the qualities the Chinese leadership tries to claim for itself.

The Chinese leadership's belief in scientism also supports a dualistic outlook. "For the committed communist," writes John Young, "it is not plurality but duality that governs the globe. Every problem, every argument, every issue resolves itself ultimately into two sides, and only two: 'a bourgeois' side and a 'socialist' side. And in these conflicts there can be no neutrals."[62] In this light, scientism supports a rigid black-and-white worldview.

As assumed by the Chinese leadership, scientism also includes a moral objective. Børge Bakken comments on the link between morality and scientism: "Under the protection of the magic spell of science, the sorcerers of modernity seem to make norms stop fluctuating, morality freezes, and 'correctness' flow abundantly in a kingdom of reason."[63] Bakken's analysis points to the danger of applying scientism in the political arena, for it highlights how scientism with its monolithic perspective cannot tolerate the complexity, fluidity, and change that characterize modern-day Chinese politics. In addition science suggests a sense of finality, which when applied to social order, amounts to permanence, a condition the government desires.

With such a rigid worldview, the Chinese leadership can only dismiss the Falun Gong movement for "spreading superstition" and cast its believers as "losers" who "cannot adjust to the fierce competition of the modern world."[64] However, the rise of Falun Gong can be read as an outcry against the prevalence of scientism in Chinese politics and the negation of human spirituality that accompanies it. Whereas scientism insists on interpreting the world through rationality, Falun Gong makes a strong attempt to know and understand the world from alternate perspectives. As Li Hongzhi says in *Zhuan Falun:* "Now the guiding ideology of human science can only limit its development and research in the material world. It walks on a road of studying a thing only after it is known. It dares not treat those phenomena which cannot be seen or touched, but which exist in a material way. 'Buddhist doctrine' can provide answers about the immeasurable and limitless world for the humankind."[65]

This passage contains a strong overtone of mystical religiosity, and Li makes it very clear his religious doctrine is an antithesis to the all-knowing scientific practice of contemporary Chinese politics. Reflecting on this view, Shang Jiuyun, a Chinese scholar from Beijing Normal University, comments, "There are always many things that are not knowable within the confines of knowledge. Thus religion has taken advantage of the way of imagination to provide a method of knowledge for humankind, to answer questions about nature, society and the human world."[66]

Shang holds that even in modern times, religion plays a useful role that cannot be usurped by science. When rational reasoning fails to provide answers or solutions to various issues, the people turn to religion to seek answers. Furthermore, in contemporary societies in particular, many religions cease to offer literal interpretations of all-encompassing truth. Rather they become agencies for believers to solve larger humane social issues. In this regard Shang and those in the Falun Gong movement are at odds with state doctrine, for even to acknowledge an alternative way of reading and understanding the world is antithetical to the entrenched perspective of scientism.

❧ THREE ❧ Why Is Falun Gong Popular?

CHINA DURING THE 1990s was in an era of postsocialism.[1] In such times communist ideology declines, and economic activities prevail. While it faced more challenges from the citizenry, the leadership clung to its old Marxist ideology and continued efforts to safeguard its legitimacy. Although economic reforms resulted in a more relaxed attitude toward spiritual liberalization, the regime resisted any political change.

Reared in a system where political conviction is viewed as nobler than material comfort and personal identity is tied to the revolutionary cause, many Chinese from the revolutionary era experienced a heavy blow to their faith when the legitimacy and credibility of the government system was called into question; changing values about the economy contradicted the Communist Party's moral justification for its actions, leaving citizens in a moral vacuum.

How do the Chinese cope with a society in flux? As Ben Xu notes, they struggle with the desire for a better standard of living, the fear of ruthless economic competition, and an unreadiness for the new pressures of commercialization. The "being after" embedded in these sentiments evokes anxiety that is sometimes tinged with a deep sense of uncertainty and nostalgia for the relative simplicity of the old ways.[2] Xu pinpoints the psychosocial state of many Chinese citizens: living in an insular and unnatural environment, they grew accustomed to a simple and routine life. The living standard was low but there were few worries. The main necessities of life—a job, health care, and housing—were provided by the government. The transition to the market economy came as a rude awakening. The opportunities and the freedom brought by the market economy, otherwise enjoyed in capitalist countries, have made the Chinese feel disoriented and overwhelmed.

The experience of Chinese citizens in an evolving economy parallels in many ways how former citizens of the Soviet Union reacted to the arrival of *perestroika* ("restructuring"). In "Late Socialism: An Eternal State," a chapter in his *Everything Was Forever,* Alex Yurchak comments on how the Soviet public reacted to *perestroika* and *glasnost* ("openness, public discussion"):

"When the policies of perestroika and glasnost were introduced in 1985, these campaigns were thought to be no different from the endless state-orchestrated campaigns before them. However, within a year or two it dawned on the Soviets that something unimaginable was taking place. Many speak of having experienced a sudden 'break of consciousness' and stunning shock."[3]

Although the reforms in China and the former Soviet Union differ in many ways and have produced disparate outcomes, the initial reactions in both countries share similarities. To citizens of both countries, the reforms symbolized a rupture in official ideological presuppositions that had conditioned and shaped their modes of thinking over several decades. Thus the initiation of reforms produced public confusion, shock, and conflict, as well as fond memories of the past. Furthermore the public experienced a strong sense of unpreparedness for, and anxiety about, the future.

Western scholars have written extensively on the impact of modernity in general, and their commentaries illuminate the Chinese situation. They explain how modernity makes an impact on big issues (such as cultural archetypes) as well as small ones (such as personal mental states). Influencing citizens more than psychologically, it reaches into the cultural presuppositions of a society, the foundation upon which a society is a built. Hans Blumenberg employs the term "angst" to describe the impact of modernity, explaining, "Each time the so-called modernity has moved further into secular history, it has inherited, and now occupies, a vast domain of enigmatic questions for which it has no answer. We must allow for the fact that any epoch may inherit questions that the culture cannot answer within the presuppositions."[4]

When China abruptly moved from its revolutionary era to an era of modern capitalism, political activities—once the major form of socialization—were replaced by commercial activities. An ideology to fit this new era has yet to evolve. When economic pursuits become the locus of sociopolitical activities, challenges to the legitimacy of the official orthodoxy, crises of faith, and the popular reception of a heterodox folk religion are the result.

Anthony Giddens and Wade Roof relate the thrust of modernity to existential issues. Roof argues that modernity makes people feel "ontologically insecure" or "ontologically uncertain."[5] Giddens elaborates by saying that a person cannot consistently feel a part of a biographical continuity if he or she is apprehensive about possible risks to his or her existence or feels morally "empty" because of the lack of a loving "self-regard."[6] The perception that the foundation of one's existence is threatened leads to physiological symptoms. The state of affairs forms the context for an alternative folk religion to perform functions that the government is unable to handle—providing moral support and relieving psychological distress.

David Apter and Tony Saich employ the terms "symbolic capital" and "economic capital"—developed during their sociological cognitive research on the Yenan revolutionary experience—to compare and contrast the ideological mainstays that undergird the two eras. Symbolic capital "offers alternative truths on which to act and promises to those who accept such truths that acting on them will transform one's own condition by altering the conditions of society at large."[7] Apter and Saich assume symbolic capital has served as the motor that has propelled the Chinese people toward a utopian vision during the years of the revolution. Under such conditions, idealistic growth needs are elevated, and material possessions and physical comfort become insignificant. The introduction of a market economy, however, altered this perception. The fantasy, signified by symbolic capital, "gives way to duller, slogging requirements of generating 'Economic Capital.'"[8] The Chinese, who once were supposed to have lived on the "nourishment of the mind" (*jingshen shiliang*), now enjoy the comfort and fulfillment of material goods. Yet, in terms of their perception of the new social setting, the transition has represented a rupture of what they are accustomed to and causes unease. When the official establishment makes "any transition from a model where symbolic capital is to be applied to economic capital, a moral vacuum is [produced]." The occurrence of a moral void is possible because "Marxism is an inversionary discourse good for criticizing and exposing the deficiencies of capitalism, [but not for offering] good solutions to the problems they expose."[9] As their discussion of symbolic and economic capital implies, that somatization (pain and illness that cannot be linked to pathological causes) is triggered by citizens' inability to reorder, reinvent, and reframe their old ontological perception to fit a shifting social reality. Having once lived in a simple, familiar, and secure society where political undertakings occupied daily life, many Chinese now feel unready to face a difficult, demanding, and chaotic social environment. They have failed to develop a coping mechanism, and it is hard for the average citizen to complete the learning curve necessary to turn into a New Economic Man. To a large extent, this dysphoria— anxiety, malaise, and discomfort—symbolizes the behavioral manifestation of ontological and cognitive disorientation.

Further evidence of the psychological changes in Chinese citizens may be found in the arts. In contemporary China, art and literature tend to be among the first media through which to express public sentiment. Known to be sensitive to the social mood, Chinese artists and authors have effectively depicted the reactions of Chinese citizens to the nation's transition to a market economy. The deepest dilemmas of the era have been captured in paintings by artists in the New Art Wave of the mid-to-late 1980s; characters and situations such as the "confused self," "hostile others," "endless waiting," "absurd reality," and "a meaningless existence associated with the routine of everyday life" abound. These artistic characters and themes are also conveyed in literature, including the fictional characters created by Bai Dao and Xu Xing or the poetic metaphors of Yang Lian and Gu Cheng.[10]

How do citizens react to the social upheaval? Statistics indicate that many feel they have descended to the bottom rung of the social ladder. Once the direct beneficiaries of the communist revolution, Chinese blue-collar workers, for example, now face massive layoffs, becoming the victims of the system that sought to elevate their status.

Chinese blue-collar workers are not the only ones to suffer from the negative consequences of modernity. Intellectuals also find it difficult to adjust to the new social environment. For example Li Yixiang, a graduate student at a top Chinese university (comparable to MIT) and a Falun Gong member, tells the story of his reaction to the new conditions: "After becoming a graduate student at Qinghua University, I was surrounded by brilliant fellow graduate students. Encountering difficulties in scientific research, I felt overwhelmed by responsibilities. I felt a great loss of self-assurance and self-esteem, and profound psychological pressure. My health then started to deteriorate."[11] Li articulates a dilemma common to many Chinese who face the new force of competition. Reared and brought up in a revolutionary era, they had enjoyed the security of the so-called iron rice bowl, a common metaphor for the guarantee of a life-long job. With the introduction of economic reforms, their iron rice bowl is taken away, and they are handed a clay rice bowl in its place—one that can be broken at any time. As a result their sense of being in control of their lives is fundamentally shattered. To them an iron rice bowl signifies security, ease of mind, and being in control— values the socialist system promised and attempted to deliver. In contrast a clay rice bowl represents instability, uncertainty, not having control of one's life, and inviability in competition—values that capitalism embodies. In short, once branded the masters of socialism, they now find themselves to have become laborers in a new, unkind economic system.

These psychological effects lead to what many perceive as the deterioration of peoples' physical health, though this weakening often lacks pathological causes. Often the decline betrays psychosocial symptoms, where psychological stress expresses itself as a physical condition caused by pressures in the external environment. To a layperson, one's perceived poor health is caused by stress brought on by a hostile environment. Arthur Kleinman proposes the term "social suffering," which he says, "takes in the human consequence of war, famine, depression, disease, torture—the whole assemblage of human problems that result from what political, economic, and institutional power does to people—and also human responses to social problems as they are influenced by those forms of power."[12] In many societies, particularly those of developing countries, symptoms can sometimes not be explained by pathological causes. In many of these cases, sociopolitical and institutional forces underpin the suffering of patients. Consequently what manifests as private and individual sickness becomes "social suffering." In this light, when conducting an analysis of somatic discourse, scholars must employ multiple tools—from interdisciplinary fields such as rhetorical criticism, cultural anthropology, medical anthropology, ethnography, and sociology of religion—to get an accurate and comprehensive reading of the somatization.

What factors are at play in the assertions—of both Falun Gong and medical professionals—that Falun Gong can "restore" the health of its members, making the remedy of the folk religion seem as effective as biomedicine? According to some medical anthropologists, healing begins to occur when patients' bodies are considered a social agency. M. L. Lyon and J. M. Barbalet explain, "Emotion has a role in social agency as it significantly guides and prepares the organism for social action through which social relations are generated. The Body cannot be seen merely as subject to external forces; the emotions which move the person through bodily processes must be understood as a source of agency: social actors are embodied."[13] The phrase "social actors are embodied" refers to how the human body, alternately viewed as "topical body," interacts with political domination of cultural activity. Examples are relations between the body and health, the body and political domination, the body and trauma, the body and religion, the body and gender, the body and self, the body and emotion, and the body and technology.[14] Thus the body is more than an existential organism of biology. Rather it represents a microcosm of the external environment, specifically connected to issues in different social domains. Problems in the body politic affect and manifest in individual bodies. Individual bodies can also exert influences on the body politic. When bodies become social, human emotion—a cognitive activity—becomes the agency. They can be negative, resulting in somatic pain, or positive, forming the basis of energy and motivation.

Contemporary psychoanalysis provides another set of lenses for viewing the somatic expression of social suffering in private bodies. According to James Jones, a person internalizes the experiences of his or her external world. These patterns, "once internalized, cannot remain totally inward but push for expression and reenactment in the external world as well."[15] Jones assumes that one's somatization is psychosocial: negative social context leaves an imprint on private bodies, which in turn has to find expression in somatic idioms. The somatic expression can also become political, bringing pressure to hegemony. Discussing the harm of internalized sentiment, Jones notes, "Because the objects of our experience are painful, we are 'compelled to internalize in an effort to control them.' But it does not work. The defense turns out to be a Trojan horse. By taking these objects inside us, they live on as 'internal saboteurs'—the conflicting camp of anxious, guilty, condemning inner voices."[16] Internalization of negative emotions can inflict profound harm on human bodies, and should be articulated and heeded.

How does Falun Gong, a folk religion, seem to have the ability to "cure" this psychological sickness, as a majority of its members claim it does? Most Falun Gong members cite "restoration of health" as the primary factor for them to become followers. Quantitative surveys also seem to confirm their assertions. According to a five-city survey conducted by eleven medical specialists from Beijing Union Hospital and ten other Chinese hospitals in October of 1998, of the 12,371 Falun Gong members they interviewed, 58 percent said they became healthy after practicing Falun Gong; 25 percent said they felt a strong improvement.[17]

Li Hongzhi's Teachings

A large number of Falun Gong members claim that what initially attracted them to this folk religion was its purported therapeutic effect on their health. Li Hongzhi, the spiritual leader of Falun Gong, professes that he does not treat the symptoms of ailing patients. Instead he goes after the root cause of the "illness"—spiritual degradation. He claims he does not provide a cure for a "sick" body in the conventional biomedical sense, rather he purifies followers' bodies so they are free of sinful karma, the source of ill health. He says, "Some people think that treating patients, curing their illnesses, and improving their health are good deeds. In my view, they have not really cured the illness. Rather, instead of removing [it], these people have either prolonged or spread the illness. To solve this problem, to really get rid of the illness, [we] must remove the [bad] karma."[18] Karma, a key concept in Li's theory, comes from the tenets of Buddhism. According to traditional Buddhism, reincarnation dominates human existence. Karma—good or bad human acts—determines what form a human will assume in his or her next life. Feng Youlan (Fung Yu-Lan) explains that "the deeds or karma of each sentient being in successive past experience[s] determine what he is to be in existence still to come. These rebirths take place on several different levels: that of the beings in the various hells, of animals, of human beings, of the divine beings in the various heavens. In their totality, they constitute the wheel of life and death."[19] When Li employs karma as a concept, it takes on a derogatory connotation. It refers to the immoral or "bad" behavior and practices of individuals. Hence it is a synonym of "black substances," or *yieli*.

Li claims karma accumulates when an individual performs unethical deeds, and consequently it constitutes the etiology of disease: "When this black substance is accumulated in great amounts, it will form a field surrounding one's body, which will wrap him inside," resulting in sickness.[20] He equates karma with "disease poison" (*bingdu*) and "germs or bacteria" (*xijun*).[21] Worse, he says, karma prevents one from believing in moral laws: "With a lot of black substance, one's enlightenment quality will be affected. Because it forms a field around one's body and wraps a person up right in the middle, one is cut off from Zhen-Shan-Ren [truthfulness, benevolence, and compassion—main tenets of Falun Gong], the characteristics of the universe. Thus, this person's enlightenment quality will be poor."[22]

At first this passage seems rather esoteric because it includes allusions to the Chinese classical tradition. Classical Chinese religious thought is characterized by three fundamental beliefs. First, when one commits immoral deeds, he or she accumulates negative qualities and is further distanced from attaining enlightenment. Second, because ceremonial rites (*li*) inherit their qualities from the universe, the source of morality, the acts in the rites incorporate this morality into human action.[23] Finally, when the universe, religious rites, and human beings are aligned in a continuum, actions in one sphere invariably affect the other two. These three principles underlie Li's major arguments. His appropriation of classical philosophical beliefs into his theory demonstrates his roots. This traditional frame of reference for his views resonates with his believers.

To reject the decline into moral degradation, Li urges practitioners to practice Zhen-Shan-Ren, which, he says, will lead them to spiritual transcendence. Only when one becomes spiritually elevated, he says, can one realize physical wellness. This claim represents the essence of Li's doctrine, and all his other theories revolve around this major premise: to reach spiritual elevation, one has to remove bad karma. He reiterates: "the bad things on your mind, the karmic field surrounding your body, and the elements that make your body unhealthy must be cleaned out. If they are not cleaned out, how can you, with such an impure, dark body and a filthy mind, practice cultivation toward a higher level?"[24] Li explicitly correlates morality and health, implying that committing sinful deeds leads to sickness and that to be healthy again, one has to become moral by believing in Zhen-Shan-Ren. To purify the body, one engages in the accumulation of *de* ("virtue," "white substance"), which Li considers the ultimate goal of moral cultivation. To acquire *de* one must do ethical deeds, endure suffering, and above all, relinquish human desire. As Li says, "Cultivation must take place through suffering so as to test whether you can part with or care less about different sentimentality and desire. If you are attached to these things, you will not succeed in cultivation. Affection among family members, love between a man and a woman, love for parents, feelings, friendship, doing things for friendship, and everything else all relate to this sentimentality. What takes over in its place is benevolence, which is something nobler."[25]

Li's belief in the elimination of human sentiment and carnal desire appears to be influenced by Taoism and Buddhism, for these ancient religious traditions commend the detachment of oneself from human interaction and society. A Taoist or a Buddhist strives to avoid all human attachment—be it love, lust, fame, fortune, popularity, or success. These classical teachings are the core tenets of Li's teachings. As he sees it, only when one is rid of mundane desires is he or she capable of engaging in spiritual cultivation. In other words only a person with a "pure" mind can participate in spiritual practice.

Li's claim that one has to suffer in order to reach spiritual elevation parallels similar beliefs throughout the world. Religious leaders and writers do not consider this type of suffering "as misery or misfortune" but, as classicist Thomas Gould claims, a "catastrophic suffering, undergone by some great figure, man or god, far in excess of the sufferer's deserts."[26] Gould assumes that suffering is "special" because it represents a sublime experience through which man and god alike can reach transcendence. Moreover religious leaders "reinvent" suffering in order to help believers to "acknowledge suffering where we normally do not see it" in order to "move emotions and alter perceptions."[27]

Drawing on classical Chinese teachings, Li argues that one "must suffer the toughest hardships of all. The other day, I said that the perception of humankind's times and space is different from the greater universe. Here, our measurement of two hours equates to a year in that space. If a person practices cultivation in this harsh condition, he will be considered truly remarkable."[28] Suffering, no longer strictly considered corporal pain, grows into a necessary stepping stone to reach enlightenment. It is a tempering process to toughen and purify the mind. Implicit in this belief is the notion that suffering is a noble undertaking, accessible only to those elected.

How is an individual capable of withstanding this suffering? Those who belong to Falun Gong, a "moral community," consider themselves the chosen, the elect; those who are outside the group are considered inherently immoral, a distinction Li stresses both to his practitioners and in his addresses to the general public. In Chinese culture a collectivity has long been the means through which people develop identity and a feeling of solidarity. Moreover collectivity enforces and practices a single ethical standard, making members of a group a virtual "moral community." In Falun Gong the moral community guides members to reframe suffering into something nobler. The sufferer is commended as being a martyr or a hero. In turn, the suffering of the group turns into a hallowed sacrifice and epic achievement.[29] Thus suffering, reconstructed in the particular discourse of a moral community, becomes an empowering agency. The collective discourse enables a member to reorder his or her perception of suffering and reinvents pain as an experience one must have in order to reach enlightenment.

Li Hongzhi's tutorial on suffering strikes a chord among members. In a statement titled "Happiness," a practitioner says, "Happiness is antithetical to suffering. One will not experience happiness if he/she has not exerted himself/herself. One will not feel the value of life if he/she has not led a life of vicissitude. I am happy, because I have found destination of life in Zhen-Shan-Ren. Falun Dafa provides me with inspirations of being unselfish, endurance and tolerance."[30]

The statement of this Falun Gong member reflects the popular feelings of many practitioners. They are inclined to consider the efficacy Li Hongzhi's discourse from an affective perspective and in concrete terms. They are attracted to Falun Gong because its belief system restores happiness and health for them. Very few of them elevate Li Hongzhi's words to a philosophical plane. Li claims to be a healer, a preacher, and a reformer. What does he do to move his believers to action? We can attempt an answer: he reinvents personal affliction and helps to mobilize his followers' will, passion, and intelligence in order to alter perceptions and change the world at large.

Members' Reception of Falun Gong Teachings

Many of those who join Falun Gong feel inspired and morally transformed by the ethical lessons espoused in Li Hongzhi's teachings. According to a research report by the Sichuan Provincial Academy of Social Sciences, Li Hongzhi's moral admonitions strike a chord with intellectuals and retired government officials. According to the report, this group tends to believe that Falun Gong teachings provide rational explanations for contemporary social issues.[31] "By reading *Zhuan Falun* many times, many practitioners came to understand [ethical] issues that have perplexed them in the past," notes one Falun Gong believer.[32] In his "Ten-Thousand-Character Open Letter to Jiang Zemin," Wang Youqun, a retired government official and Falun Gong practitioner, used the phrase "casting off one's old self and being reborn" (*tuotai huangu*) to refer to the thorough transformation Li Hongzhi's teachings are able to instigate in practitioners.[33] Or, to use an analogy Western readers are familiar with, many Falun Gong members claim they have been "twice born," a term coined by William James, in his studies of the psychology of religious experience.[34] As David Shulman and Guy G. Stroumsa explain, "Our initial birth as human beings requires, at least for the religious virtuoso, a 'second birth.' That is, some form of radical transformation, an undoing and refashioning of the person."[35]

The same experience is described from a Taoist perspective: "Hui Tzu said to Chuang Tzu: I have a big tree named ailanthus. Its trunk is too gnarled and bumpy to apply a measuring line to, its branches too bent and twisty to match up to a compass or square. You could stand it by the road and no carpenter would look at it twice."[36] Hui Tzu and Chuang Tzu are comparing the natural form of an unpruned tree with a person who has not received Taoist illuminations. Yet, after a "second birth"—reaching Taoist enlightenment—we see how a human being is transformed into a "Great Man," a virtuoso who has mastered the essence of Taoist tenets: "The Great Man in his actions will not harm others, but he makes no show of benevolence or charity. He will not move for the sake of profit, but he does not despise the porter at the gate. He will not wrangle for goods or wealth, but he makes no show of refusing or relinquishing them. He will not enlist the help of others in his work, but he makes no show of being self-supporting, and he does not despise the greedy and base. He is content to stay behind a crowd. All the titles and stipends of the age are not enough to stir him to exertion."[37] The Great Man personifies Taoist beliefs. Becoming a Taoist master requires rigorous spiritual tempering, leading to a metamorphosis from the "natural" or "unaffected" state of an individual. Such are the transformations Falun Gong members claim they have experienced.

To religious leaders, and certainly those of Falun Gong, transfiguration of a metaphysical nature is discernible and deliberate. Indeed Falun Gong leaders see their followers becoming healthier, happier people after practicing within the group. The following is one member's testimony: "Before I practiced Falun Gong, I had hepatitis B. Within six months, the illness changed from acute to chronic. I took the best Western medicine, but did not feel better. Then I came into contact with Falun Gong. The day when I heard Master Li's lecture, my appetite improved. After I started to practice Falun Gong, I stopped using medicine. It has been three years, and I am full of energy."[38] Testimonies such as this are common among Falun Gong members. Before accepting Falun Gong, they had "sick" bodies, and only when they began to engage in ethical practices espoused by Falun Gong was their health was restored. They have apparently experienced a transformation that is both mental and physical. Physically they feel healthier, and mentally they are better equipped to deal with the vicissitudes of a competitive environment.

An important factor of the Chinese worldview is at play in this religious healing. As rhetorical phrases in China suggest, many Chinese presume that a symbiotic relationship exists between the "mind" and the "body." When the mind is robust and moral, one's physical health is rehabilitated. Conventional Western biomedical concepts cannot be used to adequately explain Li's "magical touch." How does religious belief affect one's health? No surgery, pills, or traditional medical therapy is used to cure Falun Gong members. To understand Li's so-called efficacy, let us first borrow the lens of cultural studies to illuminate the "magical touch." According to Clifford Geertz, "Meanings can only be 'stored' in symbols: a cross, a crescent, or a feathered serpent. Such religious symbols, dramatized in rituals or related in myths, are felt somehow to sum up, for those for whom they are resonant, what is known about the way the world is, the quality of the emotional life it supports, and the way one ought to behave while in it. Sacred symbols thus relate to an ontology and cosmology to an aesthetic and a morality."[39]

Religious symbols are not mere motifs; nor are religious rituals mere performance arts. Rather, they are carriers of values orienting humans toward ontological and aesthetical knowledge, thereby invigorating their emotion. In such a perspective, Li's apparent healing powers contain more complex subtexts than conventionally proclaimed "paranormal abilities."

We connect Geertz's claim to the peculiar condition of contemporary China. With a primary emphasis on solidarity, Falun Gong aids members to resolve issues in their private life and social environment. They develop what Francis Hsu calls an "affective relation" in which they look to other human beings for intimacy.[40] Indeed Falun Gong's rituals facilitate unity and restore healthy interpersonal interaction. The following exemplifies this process: "Falun Gong members practice religious rituals together every day. From strangers, they become friends. The activities they do range from exchanging thoughts on practicing the ritual, to talking about one another's family, and to discussing current affairs. They care about each other, and try to help each other. As a result, mutual trust is increased, and a brotherhood and a sense of identity are established."[41] Implicit in these comments is the development of a sense of trust, a quality that had all but disappeared since the Cultural Revolution in China. Trust, as Anthony Giddens argues, is essential to human well-being because "it forms the foundation of an individual's healthy attitude to deal with the social reality. It creates a sense of ontological security that will carry the individual through transition, crises, and circumstances of high risk."[42]

The attachment Falun Gong cultivates makes it possible for members to feel that Falun Gong is their extended family as well as their caretaker. Group meetings and exercise—the daily rituals of Falun Gong—improve the quality of members' emotional lives and provide them with strength to deal with external societal issues. The external threat to their existential concerns is lessened. Don Handelman uses the term "interior stability," providing another angle for us to understand the role of emotional support members need for viability.[43]

Shang Jiuyun finds Chinese religions such as Buddhism and Taoism to be particularly therapeutic for Falun Gong members: "[Buddhism and Taoism] offer justifiable explanations about the decline of society, especially about the existence of suffering and evil. Moreover Chinese religions exhort believers to practice kindness and link human suffering with the causal effect of personal actions. They also tell members to find the cause of suffering within. As a result, members' mental endurance is solidified."[44] Shang pinpoints the cultural characteristics of Chinese religions, referring particularly to folk religions that are widely practiced. From antiquity to contemporary times, the life of the common Chinese person has been plagued by chaos, pain, frustration, and instability owing to the corruption and incompetence of the political elite. Falun Gong, like folk religions in general, provides health regimens that reinvent somatic expressions and infuse them with normative and emotional import. Here culture influences the healing of Falun Gong members as "transformation is regularly patterned and culturally determined."[45]

The Chinese Notion of Mind and Body

Most Chinese believe there is a symbiotic and organic link between the mind and the body. This belief constitutes the major premise that undergirds Li Hongzhi's claim as a healer.

To put the Chinese conception of interrelation between mind and body in proper context, one should first review how the mind and body are viewed in many parts of Western culture. In the West the mind and body are popularly considered to be the paradigms for such dualistic categories as "mind" and "matter," "form" and "matter," or "actor" and "action." This categorization treats the mind and body as unrelated entities, a dichotomization that is especially true of biomedical perception in Western medicine.[46] One sees the separation expressed in the dominant metaphor of the self, and particularly in the image of the body that "contains" the mind. In popular Western iconography, terms such as "prison house," "temple," "machine," and "instrument" are used to describe the physical human body as an outer form that houses the mind.[47] As these phrases suggest, certain traditional Western views consider the connection between the mind and body to be loose and only biologically related.

In contrast many Chinese hold a holistic view of the relationship between the mind and the body. Chinese concepts of the mind and the body tend to be couched in terms of a process rather than a duality. To treat the mind and the body as a "process" is to view each particular as a consequence of the other. In other words a human being is understood as the unity of two organic processes that require one another as a necessary condition of their mutual existences.[48] The mind and the body are like "yin and yang," "left and right," "up and down," and "self and other." Each cannot exist without the other. Epistemologically the Chinese complementary view of mind and body reflects an organic slant in Chinese culture, which posits "a world of processes characterized by interconnectedness, interdependence, openness, mutuality, indeterminateness, complementariness, correlativity, coexistence, and an environment in which continuous processes are intrinsically related to each other."[49] In contrast the Western Neoplatonic notion of separation of mind and body implies an essentialist interpretation of the world, a world of duality characterized by "discreteness, finality, closeness, determinateness, and independence; in short, this perspective assumes an environment in which one thing is related to the 'other' extrinsically."[50]

While insisting that mind and body have a connection, the Chinese do not believe the two share power equally; the mind is in control. Although it appears to mirror the Western view, this belief is distinctly different: the mind is superior, but it is still interconnected with the body; in the West the mind is merely "housed" in the body and can be "set free." Peter Boodberg corrects this notion, saying that "the intellect is the 'wellspring' or the 'fountainhead' that keeps the body nourished and firm. Intellect is the 'essence' (*qi*) of body as the concentrated form of a single reality."[51] Roger Ames goes a step further. He points out that the mind, analogous to "intellect" or "essence," is of "a higher order of being than the body, for it provides the means for human beings to pervade the cosmos."[52] Boodberg and Ames alert us to an important nuance of the Chinese conception: the mind controls the body and not vice versa. This assumption constitutes one of the major premises of classical Chinese tradition.

Classical Chinese literature is replete with the notion of the mind acting on the body. The belief in the imperceptible influence and efficacy of the mind, in which the intellect stretches across space and penetrates everywhere, is grounded in the correlative relationship between the mental and the physical, as expressed in this poem:

> The internal repository—the distilled essence is a fountainhead,
> Flood-like, placid, it is source of *qi*.
> Where this source does not dry up,
> The body will be sturdy;
> Where the fountain is not exhausted,
> The nine orifices will have clear passage;
> And one will be able to exhaust the cosmos
> And cover the earth.[53]

The noncorporeal, intangible, and imperceptible intellect is seen as capable of moving the corporeal, tangible, and perceptible world.[54] Moreover, while they are interdependent, the mind and the body, as entities, derive their strength from the universe. Another poem continues:

> The life of the human being is such
> That Heaven [*tian*] unfolds his distilled essence [*qi*];
> And earth [*di*] unfolds his form [*xing*].
> The combination of these constitutes the human being.
> Where there is concord, he lives;
> Where there is not, he does not.[55]

Though heaven and earth give form to the mind and body, all four elements maintain a positive relationship with each other.[56] When the universe operates smoothly, the human mind and body will be strong; when the universe is in discord, the human mind and body will be weak. Furthermore heaven and earth are not representative of transcendent creators who "author" humanity. Rather the human being, like all existence, is autogenerative and arises within heaven and earth.[57] To relate these beliefs to Falun Gong, Li echoes and advocates these values in his teachings. The major thesis of his theory traces the decline of physical health to the regression of the body politic, for he believes that there is a mutual influence between humanity and habitat.

These expressions of moral tutelage sum up the essence of Chinese classical philosophies of Confucianism, Taoism, and Buddhism. Morality, rites, and spiritual cultivation ground human beings. In this regard Li Hongzhi is merely following the footsteps of his forefathers; he acts as an interpreter of culture to restore morality and rehabilitate his fellow human beings.

Culturally Bound Syndromes Unbound

Having employed rhetorical criticism and medical anthropology, to discuss Falun Gong's reordering of bodily pain into a rite of passage for personal enlightenment, I shall now employ cultural anthropology to explain the role of society and culture in producing and undoing sickness. The culture of a society constructs the way its members think and feel about sickness and healing. That is to say that the members of a society are taught and conditioned by culture about different sicknesses and their names, their characteristic symptoms and courses, their causes and mitigating circumstances, and their cosmological and moral significance. A society's cultural concern with sickness and healing is known as "ethnomedicine."[58] While culture conditions how members perceive, articulate, and react to illness, it also provides alternative constructs for them to seek recovery. In this light, sickness ceases to be merely about pathogens and becomes "culturally bound," to use the term employed by Arthur Kleinman.[59]

Sociocultural effects can produce or prevent sickness, and thus perform the function Robert Hahn refers to as "mediation."[60] For example a society's culture instills in its members ideas and values relating to living conditions and hygienic care. By such guidance they are brought into greater or lesser contact with pathogenic sources; thus sickness may be fostered or prevented.[61] The same premise can be used to describe how Chinese society and culture in recent years has increased its members' exposure to psychological pain that leads to unexplained somatic complaints. The Chinese government, assuming the parental role for the extended community, is responsible for policies and practices that have produced this disorder. Hence scholars who study the spread of somatic disorder in China refer to the illness as "culturally constructed." If the society and culture surrounding an individual can introduce or create illness, it must also be possible that the community can cure itself and accept the role of caretaker—a situation Hahn calls "production."[62] Because a society's beliefs and relationship patterns produce sickness and healing, it must also be true that relationships and cultural beliefs may themselves be pathogenic or therapeutic.[63] In the Chinese context, Falun Gong, as a health regimen, offers healing of many kinds to its members, particularly for the somatic disorders brought on by stress from the modern age. Let us consider how traditional Chinese medical practice fosters social support and therapy for patients. Kleinman has found an example in how a Chinese doctor interacts with a patient and his family: "The [traditional] Chinese-style doctor spends more than double the time of his Western-style colleague explaining things to patients. He will answer questions. If the patient has a specific question about the theory behind the practice, he will attempt to explain it to him. If the patient mentions psychological problems accompanying his symptoms, the doctor will inquire about them, explain their significance, and suggest how medicine, diet, and other somatic interventions are likely to affect them. Some Chinese doctors will allow the patient and family to ventilate their anxiety. They may offer support and practical advice and perhaps, if they know them well, even help them decide how best to resolve family, job, and other interpersonal issues."[64] This consultation is more than an office visit between a medical professional and a patient. In addition to providing medical care, the doctor takes on the role of a friend and counselor. Apart from his job as a doctor, he is a caretaker who exudes warmth, trust, and support while gently guiding his patients. The Chinese doctor also functions as a cultural interpreter who gives culturally endorsed advice supporting traditional behavioral norms. The cure of a so-called illness is as much psychosocial as pathological. "With the help of such doctors, patients often claim they are cured even though a pathological cause may still exist," Kleinman notes.[65]

The Chinese doctor's role as a friend, authority, and counselor has parallels in Falun Gong practice. Li Hongzhi tells his followers: "I do not talk about healing illness here, and neither will we heal illness. As a genuine practitioner, however, you cannot practice cultivation with an ill body. I will purify your body. Purification of the body will be done only for those who come to truly learn the practice and the *Fa*."[66] The subtext to this statement implies that Li is following in the footsteps of Confucius by exhorting believers to emulate an ancestral behavioral pattern, "an act that symbolizes an ideal father-son, teacher-student, superior person-inferior person, healer-patient relationship."[67] With the guidance of a master, the patient turns onto the right path and is promised that he will become like the master.

In this regard healing, commonly assumed to be a private matter, becomes what Kleinman refers to as "cultural healing."[68] As he explains, "Cultural healing is a necessary activity that occurs to the patient, and his family and social nexus, regardless of whether the patient's disorder is affected or not, as long as the sanctioned cultural fit is established. The health care system provides psychosocial and cultural treatment for the illness. Thus, it 'heals' the illness, even if it is unable to effectively 'cure' the disease."[69]

Kleinman's comment pinpoints the efficacy of cultural healing, whether by a shaman, a traditional Chinese-style doctor, or a folk-religious leader such as Li Hongzhi. Rather than taking the approach of biomedicine, which attempts to find the cause of symptoms and treat it via biomedical intervention, traditional Chinese doctors employ an entirely different approach. They show patients how to reconsider the experience of "sickness," gently directing them to see that its root cause comes from elements in the culture, society, and interpersonal interaction. In this light a dysphoric becomes psychosocial—an affective disorder—which can be reversed only by providing patients with the skills to view and handle cultural and social issues. When patients recover, they are better able to meet the demands of culture and society.

Theorists such as Donna Haraway object to the consideration of the body as a naturalized and existentialized product of biology. Rather she believes the body is transformed from object to agent when biology is no longer a monolithic objectivity.[70] How does a natural body turn into an agent capable of change? When a body becomes a social body, it represents domains of cultural activity.[71] Or as Nancy Chen argues, a breathing space becomes a social space free from the control of hegemony, and within it the body can be empowered and socially disruptive.[72]

Considering this issue from the vantage point of the sociology of religion, Handelman notes the intricacies of self-transformation—how a natural body turns into a social body: "Change occurs when someone is changed. Radical personal change, self-transformation, occurs when the person takes himself apart, thereby opening the way to possible reconfiguration of existential being of selfness."[73] A personal transformation never takes place in one instant. Rather, it is a gradual process wrought with internal conflicts, reflexivity, and relapses before a new self emerges. On the role that citizens play in public spaces, Philip Wander's theory of "Third Persona" is instructive. Though he is a critic of Western critical rhetorical theory, his concept of subcultural groups as nonsubjects in public discourse sheds light on the case study of Falun Gong. Similar to the U.S. subcultural groups Wander describes, Falun Gong, as a religious dissident group, belongs in the category of "it." Such groups are traditionally "negated through the text—the language, the speaking situation," which are shaped by official orders.[74] Falun Gong's attempt to enter the public arena indicates its determination to step away from its allocated space on the periphery in order to take center stage in public discourse.

Falun Gong's attempt to change from a nonsubject to a central subject is also closely connected with its efforts to redefine religion. Roof refers to religious believers' attempts to reinvent faith as "reframing," which occurs when religious speech or symbols are used not to convey some transcendent truth but instead to *create* truth or *provoke* confrontation with it. Rather than looking on symbols as fixed realities in some objective manner, these believers see symbols as negotiated and situational, used to construct a set of meanings in the face of serious human dilemmas and existential concerns.[75]

In the contemporary era, religious followers are changing their perceptions of religious tenets and less often thinking of them as intangible higher truths. Religious symbols are taking concrete form and becoming instruments with which people can tackle problems in culture and society. This transformed mentality replaces old interpretations with a credo that is designed to make an impact on humanitarian issues. In Falun Gong, religious beliefs serve only as a medium to connect believers; it is the undertone critiquing the body politic asserts itself in Falun Gong's principles and actions.

In this regard Western sociologists' notion of culture as a toolbox is relevant to this discussion. The metaphor of a "symbolic toolbox," which is often applied to religion, suggests that people may draw selectively from its contents and exercise considerable agency in its interpretation.[76] Marsha Witten offers an example to support this argument: "For contemporary Christians, the symbol of the cross may no longer plausibly refer to the accounts of the crucifixion and resurrection of Jesus as they appear in the gospels. Yet the cross may take on significance in another way as speakers use it to condense and dramatize notions of suffering and its transcendence, or overwhelming love, or the possibilities of human transfiguration."[77]

Religious symbols may be treated as cultural tools that apply to different problems across various situations. What was formerly a sacred sign is now used as a practical instrument that serves personal interests. While classical cultural texts function as moral touchstones to redirect Falun Gong members to the path of morality, they may also be reframed, reinvented, and reordered to tackle contemporary sociocultural concerns. Many contemporary religious believers depart from finding redemption in another world in order to focus on human transfiguration in the world they inhabit. This "mega-perspective," as Handelman calls it, allows Falun Gong members to transcend inwardly directed self-interest to focus on societal issues, becoming social or cultural agents. When one is in pursuit of higher truth, firm faith and boundless energy are released. This may explain why Falun Gong members hold steadfast to their beliefs when confronted with suppression. Handelman has said that the "continuous emergence of selfness from within its sociality as the generation of an interior mega-perspective. Recursivity shapes and reshapes selfness, braiding together the possibility of selves that emerge from the possibilities of selves."[78]

✠ FOUR ✠ As Powerful as Weapons

The Use of Tropes as
Ideological Instruments

WHEN TRADITIONS ARE passed down, questions can arise concerning how later generations interpret the intentions of the people who established these customs. Do subsequent teachings remain faithful to the original vision of the classics? To use Benjamin Schwartz's term, do they recapture that vision in its "pristine freshness"? Or do the teachings fall victim to one-sidedness or distortion? The answer is neither. The redeployment of tradition in a modern context is never an issue of either/or. Rather social actors strategically choose classics as rhetorical tools to resolve the exigency of the so-called rhetorical situation.[1] Hayden White places tradition in perspective when he points out that historians always attempt to exercise "cognitive control" over the "prefiguring experience" of history. As he explains, "The 'overall coherence' of any given 'series' of historical facts is the coherence of the story, but this coherence is achieved only by a tailoring of the 'facts' to the requirements of the story form."[2] Using tradition in a "copy and paste" manner to fit a modern context will result in an incongruity between history and current affairs. Contemporaries have to modify and adjust history so it serves modern agendas. It is common practice for a contemporary religious practitioner, for example, to "redirect" theological concepts to "new referents" within their own social sphere.[3]

While it is true that cultural and sociopolitical conditions have undergone massive transformations in modern times, it is the new trends in human epistemology that govern societal change. Therefore history has to be reframed in order to be a fitting instrument for the practice of contemporary social players. F. W. Dillistone views the interrelationship between tradition and modern history more metaphorically. According to him, the calculated use of tradition exists as a mediator among content, modern thoughts, form, and history: "Man is an inveterate experimenter. He denies that the form of the container has absolute validity. He breaks through in order to explore, he breaks down in order to exploit. He conceives a dream or a vision or a hope and seeks to translate it into the outward realization. This is the 'energy' of creativity and change."[4]

While the form (history) might be old and unchanging, the enunciation of content becomes a creative human exercise. Therefore contemporary social players make studied attempts to tinker with the classics to suit their ends. While they regard classical texts as primers to guide their modern actions, their use of ancients as ideological tropes is never literal but deliberate and thoughtful so that new purposes are served.

The contemporary Chinese rhetorical experience serves as a case study to illuminate how modern social players such as the Falun Gong movement and the Chinese government treat the classics as a "toolbox" from which they choose appropriate implements to resolve new issues.[5] Endowed with a five-thousand-year-old tradition, the Chinese are especially adept at using classics in contemporary settings to achieve desirable goals. Known for being well-versed in ancient wisdom, they often employ classics as tropes to mediate human consciousness and social reality. Not only state leaders and scholars, but also common people, are familiar with traditional myths, folklore, fables, and analogues, and they regularly cite or allude to these stories in order to explicate contemporary situations.

Chinese scholars argue that many tropes used by contemporaries have cultural roots. For example Ge Gao and Xiaosui Xiao call *yuan* a "native Chinese concept."[6] Xing Lu identifies historical roots in the deployment of tropes: "The use of metaphor is a recurring rhetorical technique in Chinese literary and historical texts."[7] Analogy, considered as a popular figure of speech, is "closely related to unique Chinese cultural factors and might be special cultural 'products' of Chinese culture," argues Yingqin Liu.[8] Indirect communication is a common rhetorical device among Asians.[9] William Gudykunst and Stella Ting-Toomey explain how it functions: "The direct and indirect style refers to the extent speakers reveal their intentions through explicit verbal communication. The indirect verbal style refers to verbal messages that camouflage and conceal speakers' true intentions in terms of their wants, needs, and goals in the discourse situation."[10]

On Western notions about the function of tropes, Frank Brown notes, varieties of experiences and reflections important to religion have an intrinsic connection with poetry and poetics—a connection best understood when one pays special attention to metaphor (broadly conceived).[11] The world mediated through human discourse is never the same as the one mediated through poetry and myth.[12] William Franke provides the explanation that metaphor has become a topic onto which all the classical philosophical ontology and epistemology are projected and appear in new and specific linguistic light.[13]

The beneficial nature of tropes is not lost on social players in contemporary China. Both Li Hongzhi and Communist leaders employ tropes extensively in their discourse. Major figures of speech used by Li Hongzhi include analogy, metaphor, metonymy, and indirect communication. Making use of tropes in his speech, Li attempts to inspire pathos in his audience, to "move" them from a mundane existence to a higher plane of morality. In contrast Communist leaders resort to key words or ideographs in their political communications with the Chinese people. Ideographs, working as ideological instruments, are used across political situations to evoke uniform behavior in the people.

Tropes as Ideological Instruments for Falun Gong

Like many Chinese, Li Hongzhi skillfully uses classics to convey his theological messages. In particular he employs classical terms to serve a profound moral purpose rather than merely to preach. He encodes his contentious messages in the guise of classical maxims, archetypal myths, and allegories in order to promote his ideological agenda and propose an alternative moral discourse. This strategy frequently appears in his writing, which is similar to his preaching. Consider an example: "Some people say: 'When a Tao is one foot tall, a demon will be one yard high' (*do gao yi chi, muo gao yi zhang*). This is a false statement made by common people. A demon will never be higher than a Tao. Every time our universe goes through a period of a great many years, it always experiences a great catastrophe that destroys everything in the universe. After the new universe is reconstructed by the great-enlightened beings at an extremely high level, [they] build the universe according to their own characteristics and standards."[14]

There is a strong seditious message in this passage. Li's challenge to the official establishment is reflected in his frequent allusions to *kalpas* (*jienan*), a major belief in classical heterodox religious groups in China, particularly the White Lotus. *Kalpas* refers to universal destruction and cosmic reconstitution; it contains strong moral implications for the modern world because it assumes the existing order, its ethical norms, and sociopolitical institutions are finite, mutable, and destined to be replaced.[15] Such discourse is considered subversive because it contests the long-held Communist assumptions that moral norms rest on assumptions of stability and continuity. In Li Hongzhi's view, norms can be effective only when they are in sync with the cosmos. Humans must practice morality to ensure the smooth operation of moral order.

Li has rarely criticized the Chinese government openly, at least in his pre-exile years. Instead he has appropriated classics as metaphors—shown in his use of *kalpas*—and makes use of the implicit moral underpinnings to insinuate the failings of the official order and to promote his own agenda. Rhetorically the use of classical idioms to create common frames of reference for his audience is an effective means of persuasion as it engenders identification and conviction. For example, as William Franke explains, "Metaphor is, in effect, perceptible only as a derivative and deviant use of an expression." The metaphor always invents "its own world and objects rather than referring to things that already exist without it." Therefore a metaphor is "defined only in terms of what it negates, rather than in terms of what it positively designates."[16] Franke's comments shed light on Li's rhetorical methodology. Though Li rarely challenged the orthodoxy of the official establishment openly when he resided in China, his teachings are incendiary because they draw on deviating figures of speech such as *kalpas*. By using this rhetorical scheme, he has attempted to finish what Brett Miller calls "the metaphorical transaction with a *perspective* we were once without."[17]

Another strategy Li employs to establish the contemporary relevance of his teachings is his ironic use of officially sanctioned political terminology. For example, he says, "[If] every one of us cultivates his inner self, examines his own *xinxing* (mind-nature) to look for the causes of wrongdoing in order to improve the future, and considers others first when taking any action, human society would become better and ethical standards would rise again. The *Spiritual Civilization* would also become better and so would public security."[18]

"Spiritual Civilization" is a popular Chinese Communist term referring to the reform of people's minds and morality. The term is often used in contrast to "Material Civilization," which is synonymous with capitalism and modernity. By always pairing the two terms together, the Chinese leadership hopes to place an emphasis on the need to engage in "Spiritual Civilization" and to counter the popular Chinese perspective that "Material Civilization" should be the primary goal in the modernization drive of the nation.

The use of these symbiotic terms by the official establishment warrants special investigation. In *Doing Things with Words in Chinese Politics*, Michael Schoenhals has discussed how the Chinese leadership exercises direct control over political discourse by way of centralized management and manipulation of "appropriate" and "inappropriate" formulations. By proscribing some formulations while prescribing others, they set out to regulate what is being said and what is being written—and by extension what is being done.[19]

The Chinese government has been able to maintain its governance by means other than coercion. Its political discourse, particularly its ability to use highly formulated and coded language, has worked as an unobtrusive, subtle but effective, means of persuasion to regulate the thoughts of the Chinese people. The deployment of "spiritual" and "material" civilizations is a good example of this strategy. The Chinese people are given a lesson: modernization is a two-pronged drive; material modernization is only one part, the lesser part, and it can be guided or superseded only by spiritual modernization (Communist ideology). In the Chinese public discourse, such symbiosis is assumed to be implicitly understood.

From a rhetorical perspective, Li's use of these terms entails two primary considerations. First he uses the official message in an "inverted" manner as analogues to promote his ideological beliefs. He demonstrates that he and his followers are engaged in improving Chinese society—a move that parallels the intentions of the official establishment. Second, by using officially sanctioned terminology in his public addresses, he shows the government and public that his actions and those of his followers are consistent with officially designated behavior. Here he employs a rhetorical strategy to "borrow" the ethos from the texts of more established institutions in order to bolster his authority and ideology.

Analogy is another rhetorical device that Li uses extensively in his writings. Since most of his believers are not well educated, the evocation of vivid images is far more forceful than the use of abstract words. Li acts as "a cartographer of the inner world of his listeners: He gives form to the inchoate yearnings of their sensibilities. For him faith is an act of sensibilities, not of belief. It is a commitment of the acting, the feeling, the intelligent and the passionate body."[20] Consider Li's discussion on the consequence of not promoting morality: "If humans do not have virtue, natural calamity and man-made crises will occur. If the earth does not have virtue, all living things will wither. If the heaven does not have *Tao*, the earth will crack and the sky will cave in. When the Law is upheld, the universe is straight, and all life will be vital and vigorous. When heaven and earth are strengthened, the Law will last forever."[21]

Li correlates the consequences of immorality with the decline of the natural world. The analogy he uses between the human moral order and the rise or fall of the natural world is consistent with his fundamental belief in the supremacy of the cosmic order in human affairs. Morality ceases to be a mundane and individual act. Rather it is a mandate from the cosmos; upholding or abandoning morality will impact the operation of the cosmic order. Li thus effectively transfers the popular reverence for the cosmos to the promotion of moral regeneration. Moreover there is a rhetorical consideration in his use of analogy. By using images of "withering," "cracking," "caving in," and "vitality and vigor in life," he creates powerful word pictures to drive home for his listeners the importance of morality.

According to Li, when practitioners are in the early stages of cultivation, their "*gong* is locked up." But when they have reached the stage of Unlocking Gong (*kaigong*) and are enlightened, "it is like a bomb: It will explode and open up all supernormal abilities, all locks in the body, and hundreds of energy passes. 'Bang,' everything will be shaken open."[22] This choice of words is forceful and inspires one to action; language like this, in the words of Waddell and Dillistone, "rouses the faculties to act."[23]

Li Hongzhi also resorts to the use of metonymy to facilitate the understanding of his teachings, employing key words as symbols. For example he uses words and phrases such as "*qigong* and physical exercises," (*qigong yu tiyu*), "mindfulness" (*yinian*), "a clear and clean mind" (*qingjingxin*), and "enlightenment" (*wu*) in an attempt to compound the power of his core teachings. For example, in a section titled "A Clear and Clean Mind," he says, "The reason you cannot achieve tranquility is because your mind is not empty, and you have not reached that high level. In genuine cultivation, one must cultivate the heart: only when you upgrade your *xinxing* can you attain a clear and clean mind, and a state of free of intentions (*wuwei*), assimilate the characteristics of the universe, and remove different human desires, attachments and other bad things."[24] This passage incorporates the key words he uses repeatedly, lending force to his core concepts. Throughout his *Zhuan Falun* (The Turning Wheel of Law) are passages containing the same set of key words. While Li tends to develop complex theories, the repeated terms help the reader to understand his teachings. He starts his preaching using simple ideas, goes on to discuss complex religious and philosophical topics, and in the end invariably returns to the discussion of something simple. By using this rhetorical strategy, he provides easy access to his theories while guiding his followers to achieve a profound and long-lasting understanding.

Li Hongzhi also uses ontological metaphors. George Lakoff and Mark Johnson define "ontological metaphors" as rhetorical structures that help us in "understanding our experiences in terms of objects and substances" and that "[allow] us to pick parts of our experience and treat them as discrete entities or substances of a uniform kind. Once we can identify our experience as entities or substances, we can refer to them, categorize them, group them, and quantify them—and, by this means, reason about them."[25] For example personification is an ontological metaphor that treats an object as a person. Personification allows us to comprehend a wide variety of experiences with nonhuman entities by assigning these things human motives, characteristics, and activities that we can consider alongside our own motivations, goals, actions, and characteristics. In Li's teachings abstract concepts of moral cultivation are given human attributes to facilitate comprehension. For example he uses personification to refer to someone who has achieved enlightenment and moral cultivation: "A person with great inborn quality (*da genqi zhiren*) must first have a great amount of *de* and a very large field of this white substance. Meanwhile, this person should be able to endure the toughest hardships of all. He must have a mind of great forbearance too and be able to sacrifice. He must be able to preserve *de* as well, and have good enlightenment quality."[26]

We can draw several implications from this example of personification. The "person with great inborn quality" (hence "the person") personifies the core values Li Hongzhi promotes. Li converts nonhuman qualities to human attributes so that followers can make connections between the two. In other words, by personifying his core values, Li treats them as entities. Such an entity, in the words of Lakoff and Johnson on metaphors, "allows [believers] to refer to it, quantify it, identify a particular aspect with it, sees it as a cause and acts with respect to it."[27] Li Hongzhi creates "the person" to draw a contrast to what he terms "everyday people" (*changren*). In Li's view "everyday people" are immoral and filled with human attachments. The goal of Falun Gong is to transform followers from everyday people to moral people. "The person" thus forms the antithesis of everyday people, someone who has achieved the ultimate enlightenment. Every society and all social groups have role models. Falun Gong is no exception. "The person" is meant to be a prototype for believers to follow. But more important, Li Hongzhi creates "the person" in such a way that readers are reminded of a sage, the most virtuous person, who resides above the defiled world, free from all human attachments, and suffers in order to save humanity. By creating "the person" in the image of a sage, Li lifts "the person" above the plane of humanity. Once followers reach the high ground of morality, they follow in the footsteps of "the person" and become the "elect."

Li's most notable rhetorical strategy is his use of indirect communication—a Kierkegaardian term. As James Whitehill explains, "The intention of an indirect communication is to confront the receiver with an artistic configuration of human existence in such a way that a rigorous demand is set before him: That he responds to the configuration by *choosing himself in a positive or negative relation to it.*"[28]

Indirect communication is an effective rhetorical device in which the sender presents the receiver with a message reconfigured in issues of broad concern to humanity. A believer is "guided" to transcend his or her parochial private preoccupations in order to move toward larger human concerns. By using indirect communication, the sender attempts to construct a relationship with the receiver so that they appear to be "free of each other."[29] The so-called freedom between the sender and the receiver is possible because the sender purposely designs a "suspended" time period between the receipt of the message and subsequent action so that the receiver will engage in "deep" reflection independent of the influence of the sender. It is also possible for the receiver to engage in "independent" contemplation because he or she is able to incorporate the external environment—culture—as an additional factor in understanding a religious text: "The individual's representation of God emerges from the tension between her own private experience and the images and metaphors for God provided by her culture."[30] Acting as a catalyst, indirect communication activates religious reflection by mediating the tension between the sender's intention, private imagination, and the impact of the external environment.

Whitehill uses the term "subjective possibility" to refer to the deep thinking that indirect communication produces in a listener. Indirect communication is like a powerful stage play. It draws the audience into the "existence-possibility" on stage, and it leaves them in deep self-reflection after the curtain descends.[31] Similarly a religious message is incomplete when delivered by the religious leader; the listener is given the responsibility to complete it, meaning that he or she has to fulfill his or her part to comprehend, digest, reorder, and use it. The theater analogy may be used to refer to how a religious text serves as a literary device: "The incompleteness demands of the playgoer that he becomes co-creator of the play, slowly drawn into infusing himself, as subjectivity, through the play, filling its essential silences and naming its un-nameables with his secret voice, his own secret name. The playgoer is the end of the play: He completes it."[32]

Li Hongzhi adopts indirect communication in his teachings to exhort his practitioners to reach moral elevation. Yet he perceives himself to be a teacher, providing grammar for practitioners to find the right path. In other words, though he guides, his followers have to take the initiative to fulfill moral obligations on their own. Moreover he leaves room for them to mediate or negotiate with their innermost thoughts—their inclination to cling to old ways and their struggle to form a new self. Once their attitude changes, it is expected to be spontaneous and permanent. He says, "When you have not developed [your own] *xinxing*, whoever wishes to endow it upon you will be unable to do so, because it [has to] come completely from one's own cultivation and from cultivation of one's own mind. You can only elevate morally by developing *gong* solidly, improving yourself constantly, and assimilating to the characteristic of the universe."[33]

Li Hongzhi hopes that practitioners will exert themselves to rid themselves of mundane desires. Self-improvement is essential. A critical point in this process is the formation of an ethical "self-schemata"—a cognitive process that affects how one perceives him/herself and his/her social world.[34] With such efforts, the metamorphosis from the mundane to the ethical is presumed to be complete.

Li uses a variety of tropes as ideological instruments to promote his agenda. In an illiberal society, where dissent is prohibited, he has to resort to these rhetorical devices to encode his messages in order to circumvent censorship.

The late Chinese leader Mao Zedong once coined the term "sugar-coated bullet"[35] to refer to how political opponents encrypt their inflammatory messages in order to—as Mao saw it—deceive and harm the populace. Mao's concern is legitimate: For a people acculturated in reading between the lines, encoded messages are never lost on them.

Tropes as Aides to Communist State Machinery

On July 29, 1999, a week after Falun Gong was outlawed, the People's Republic of China Ministry of Public Security issued a warrant for the arrest of its leader, Li Hongzhi. Within three months of that day, the government had not only forged consensus but also had successfully executed a comprehensive program for the arrest of the group's top leaders, the conversion and rehabilitation of more than three hundred thousand Communist Party members who renounced Falun Gong, and the reeducation of two million rank-and-file Falun Gong practitioners.

Apart from the use of the state machinery that suppressed the Falun Gong movement by force, the reeducation of the majority of Chinese citizens has been largely carried out discursively by official propaganda. The first key term, which the government uses frequently, is "stability" (*wengding*). To "sustain stability" is the chief slogan of the government in any period when it wants to end political dissent, including the suppression of Falun Gong. In an August 1999 editorial titled "Cancer of the Society and Curse of the People," the *People's Daily* asserted, "Stability is political; stability is the essence; and stability overrides everything. This is the consensus of our Party and our people. Li Hongzhi and his Falun Gong negate the law, ignore the interest of the people, and attempt to instigate serious disturbances."[36]

To understand what the government means when it uses the term "stability," one has to know about the contrasting term, "disturbances" (*dongluan*), which has come to be associated with the rise of dissident movements. The term was first used to describe the Cultural Revolution, which is now synonymous with "Grand Disturbances of Ten Years."[37] It was used again more recently in reference to the Student Pro-Democracy Movement, as reported by a 1989 *People's Daily* editorial titled "We Must Take a Clear-Cut Stand Against Disturbances": "Flaunting the banner of democracy, they undermined democracy and the legal system. Their purpose was to sow dissension among the people, plunge the whole country into chaos and sabotage the political situation of stability and unity. This is a planned conspiracy and disturbance."[38] In contrast to "disturbances," "stability" refers to the period of economic reforms when Chinese citizens enjoy prosperity.

Hayden White argues that plot structure "plays upon our presumed, but formally unevoked, capacities to 'track' the events related in the story and, subconsciously, to 'decode' their subliminally encoded structure as a *particular kind of story.*"[39] With the use of the key term "stability" and its contrasting term "chaos," the government seems to raise a rhetorical question: In the face of chaos, do we want stability and prosperity, or do we want to return to the chaotic time of the Cultural Revolution? When faced with such a question, collective memory is invoked. The diachronic nature—the etymological roots—of this set of terms is recognized, and attitudes are changed accordingly, as many contemporary Chinese lived through the ten years of Cultural Revolution and still retain vivid memories of that chaotic period.

The second key term is "political struggle" (*zhengzhi douzheng*), which appears in another *People's Daily* from August 1999: "The struggle between our party and Falun Gong is a serious ideological and political struggle. It concerns the basic faith of our Communist Party members. It is related as well to the ideological foundation of our people to unite and strive. It pertains to the future of our party and our nation."[40] A "political struggle" is a recurring phrase that the Chinese leadership uses to characterize any dissent. It in effect attributes the opposition with having a political nature and draws a line between the government and its political opposition. Classifying Falun Gong as evil and illegal instead of benign was one of the most important discursive moves in suppressing the movement.[41] John Powers and Meg Lee raise the argument of categorization: "[The] larger repertoire of category labels is important in human conflict situations because once a phenomenon is placed into a category of 'equivalents,' people tend to treat the individual instance so labeled as they would any other member of the category."[42] In an authoritarian society, labeling is an effective tool to quash dissent and divide citizens. Two camps are drawn: us (the party) and them (the enemy). The Chinese people are then compelled to choose the government's side to protect themselves. This rhetorical strategy was employed during the Yenan Rectification Campaign, the Anti-Rightist Campaign, the Cultural Revolution, the Tiananmen Democracy Movement, and the Anti–Falun Gong Campaign. In each of these campaigns, the Chinese leadership employed the same strategy of polarization and isolation of the dissident, thus successfully rallying citizens to it cause.[43]

The third key term used to characterize Falun Gong is "cult" (*xiejiao*). According to a December 1999 *People's Daily* editorial titled "Law Must Defeat Cult," "In contemporary society, whether [a cult] is Branch Davidian or Falun Gong, whether it occurs in Europe and in the United States, it is the product of a historical period."[44] By branding a folk religion as a cult, the Chinese leadership effectively established a boundary between religion and cult.[45] Powers and Lee analyze the key word "cult" from another perspective, arguing that the government uses analogy to link Falun Gong with cults in foreign countries. Based on the claimed similarities, the arguer supports the notion that Falun Gong should be treated like the Branch Davidians,[46] and thus China is justified in suppressing the "cult" of Falun Gong.

Together key words such as "stability," "political struggle," and "cult" take on a synchronic character, working as a unit to support an ideological theme. All suggest why the government is justified in suppressing Falun Gong: Falun Gong is a cult, threatening the physical and mental well-being of the public and launching a political struggle against the government and the people. It thus becomes a public enemy. This set of key words, employed in every political campaign, becomes the common frame of reference for the people and unifies them linguistically.

Related to all the key words discussed so far is the term "support" (*zhichi*), as in the assertion that citizens support the government's decisions to suppress Falun Gong. Not long after the government outlawed Falun Gong, a news report in the July 24, 1999, issue of *People's Daily* stated: "After they read the party's decision to ban Falun Gong, people from all over the country [expressed] their support for the government to adopt such decisive measures. They argue that, because Falun Gong spreads superstitions, negating truth and science, it poses danger to the nation and people."[47] "People support the government"—a key phrase in times of political dissent—is used in all political campaigns to create the illusion of universal support for the legitimacy of the government. As Philo Wasburn notes, "These abstract symbol systems are social products whose history must be understood in order to have a full grasp of their meaning."[48] The creation of a symbolic universe is made possible with a set of symbols, whose meanings are recognizable by those who live in it. The key terms employed as part of the government's rhetorical strategy to solicit support do not work in isolation. They work as a unit to promote the major theme that the government is justified to suppress dissent. As most of the citizens have been acculturated in the communist political culture, their reaction to these key terms is analogous to how they treat cultural repertory. Assumptions are accepted without justifications. Implicit and hidden messages are recognized, and allusions are understood. The key terms become part of the major political vocabulary.

The last key phrase is the assertion that the government "creates a civilized and scientific social environment" (*yingzao wenming he kexue de shehui huanjing*) for the Chinese people in contrast to the pseudoscience and superstition promoted by Li Hongzhi. Another August 1999 *People's Daily* editorial asserts: "To create a civilized and scientific social environment, we should use Li Hongzhi as our negative teacher (*fanmian jiaoyuan*) and his Falun

Dafa as negative teaching materials. We must educate our cadres and masses with scientific knowledge and scientific spirit. We should help the masses to differentiate between what is science and what is pseudoscience. What is the promoting traditional culture and what is peddling feudal dross."[49]

As the government perceives it, science presides over all matters. In an article commenting on Jiang Zemin's *On Science and Technology*, Jiang is quoted as saying: "Science and technology are the first productive force. We must insist on putting science and technology in a strategic position, and build our nation into a prosperous one with science and technology."[50] Jiang explicated well the official policy toward science.

For the government the term "science" assumes a certain level of symbolism. It denotes what the government and Falun Gong each stand for: the government represents "light" and "civilization," terms that are associated with "science," whereas Li Hongzhi's Falun Gong stands for "darkness," "barbarism," and "pseudoscience," terms that are associated with superstition. As Liu Xiaoting notes, science ceases to be a branch of human knowledge and becomes a criterion to judge opinion, draw conclusions, and measure right and wrong. It becomes an end rather than a tool.[51]

Science has certainly become a new major ideograph in the political discourse of the Chinese government in recent times. Replacing the old party slogan calling on the Chinese people to strive for "socialism," to build a scientific world has become the new national goal. It represents how the government expresses its legitimacy. Because of the positive attributes one associates with the scientist, the Chinese government claims to have won the mandate to administer leadership.

Li Hongzhi and the Chinese government both see the need to employ tropes to promote their ideologies. But their approaches are quite different. Li Hongzhi is inclined to look to Chinese culture for tools to promulgate his beliefs and teachings. As someone well versed in classics, he understands that appropriating traditional culture provides an effective means of conveying a message. For him tradition becomes a political instrument; it lends him moral appeal in the advancement of his ideology.

The Chinese government, however, employs its rhetorical strategies differently. Through various political campaigns, it has developed a set of artificial, ritualized, and highly effective political idioms to prescribe desirable behavior and quash dissent. Since they are used repeatedly, the assumptions undergirding the terms are identified and recognized, and understanding is achieved by Chinese citizens. The use of these terms makes clear how ideological unity is accomplished.

However, the rhetorical strategies of Falun Gong and the Chinese leadership have their commonalities. In both instances political discourse is often carried out in partial terms. The propagandists employ enthymeme to evoke the historical meanings that come to be associated with these terms. They rely on their audience to complete reasoning with the help of knowledge and prior experience. And the audience, being politically acculturated, is in turn adept at recognizing the assumptions and producing the desired reactions.

❦ FIVE ❦   "Wildfire won't wipe it out—Spring wind blows it back"

The Transfiguration of
the Political Sensibility
of the Chinese People

ONCE IT ASSUMED POWER in 1949, the Chinese Communist leadership implemented an efficient political-socialization process that was successful until the introduction of economic reforms in 1978. This socialization process involved the cultivation of new patterns of behavior as well as the synchronization of beliefs and attitudes of the masses to those of the official orthodoxy. The leadership's ideological inculcation was so unobtrusive and effective that its espoused beliefs became "common sense" for the Chinese citizens. Ann Swidler defines "common sense" as "the set of assumptions so unselfconscious as to seem a natural, transparent, undeniable part of the structure of the world."[1] In other words the inculcation of Communist values into the citizenry of post-1949 China was successful to the point that an "ontological oneness" was achieved. This phrase has epistemological, cognitive, and behavioral connotations. Epistemologically the masses learned to reorder and recategorize their perception of experiences and objects in the social world; cognitively they formed a new pattern of thinking; and these epistemological and cognitive transformations ultimately led to behavioral conversion.

"Common sense" is largely created by official political discourse, and "ontological oneness" signifies the realization of a "linguistic unity" between the political elite and the masses. Consequently, for the twenty-nine years between 1949 and 1978, the Chinese people remained faithful to the Communist cause.

However, things changed in 1978. With the initiation of a market economy, a shift occurred in the leadership's public rhetoric. To justify its governance, the leadership had to make an extensive effort to consider ethos in its speech making. Concurrently the Chinese people began to metamorphose from "true believers" into a people with emerging political sensibilities. These transformations should not be viewed as unrelated snapshots of a certain time period. Rather one must observe the larger linearity of historical progress. In this light we should not consider the following discussion as an empirical historical review of different political events in contemporary China but as a rhetorical analysis of a diachronic process of germination of the Chinese people's political views from the politically fervent Red Guards, through the introspective Pan Xiao generation, to the independent-minded Shekou Youths—the background to the development of Falun Gong.

Red Guards: The Young Revolutionary Generation

The Cultural Revolution of 1966–76 is a testament to the ultimate success of the political socialization of the elite. Under the direction of the central leadership, the entire nation was galvanized to "declare a war on the 'Old World,'" so as to "build a very revolutionary [New] World."[2] During this period of tumultuous and protracted political fermentation, the Red Guards played an instrumental role in the political transformation. As one Red Guard said, "[We] will swing a big stick, demonstrate magic (*xian shentong*), exhibit supernatural power (*shi fa*), turn heaven and earth upside down; [in order to bring about fundamental changes to the old world], we are going to throw men and horses off their feet, make flowers wither so that they flow away with the water. We want to heap chaos upon chaos."[3]

At first this passage sounds like the statement of an anarchist; yet on a closer examination, it articulates the Red Guard's sense of duty in the assumed role of an agent of history. As an example of how young people become "New Revolutionary Men," consider an example from another communist nation, Cuba. In his *Transformation of Political Culture in Cuba*, Richard Fagen explains, "The Cuban effort is embedded in and draws meaning from a symbol system in which images of struggle and utopia loom large. By means of the evolving ideology of 'the new man,' the day-to-day world is linked with visions that are more global, abstract and lasting."[4] In Cuba and China instances of the official discourse take on a messianic tone. Youths are led to believe that they are the "chosen" and the "enlightened" ones who must initiate change in an otherwise "reactionary" world. The leadership's desire to turn youths into revolutionaries converges with the eagerness of youths to join the political movement. Erik Erikson looks at this issue from the perspective of youth psychology: "The search for a new and yet reliable identity can perhaps best be seen in the persistent adolescent endeavor to define, redefine, and over-define themselves and each other in often ruthless comparisons."[5] The youth strives to achieve a sense of what Erikson calls "wholeness"—the trait of basic trust. Sustaining such "wholeness" depends on the support the young individual receives from the social groups that are significant to him: his class, his nation, and his culture.[6]

Relating Erikson's critique to Chinese youths, one sees how society, symbolizing a collective goal promulgated in the official discourse, plays a crucial role in molding their individual identities by appealing to their senses of self-importance and duty. Mao Zedong made the following remarks to the Red Guards: "Your action indicates that you are expressing hatred and denunciation of landowners, the bourgeoisie, imperialism, revisionists, and their running dogs who exploit workers, peasants, revolutionary intellectuals, and parties. Your actions also suggest that your rebellion against the counterrevolutionaries is justified. You have my warmest and fullest support."[7]

In the capacity of a revered leader, Mao provided the reassurance and affirmation youths constantly seek when they engage in political action. He created the illusion of wholeness for them. The ideologue, as a seer, gives a simple rationale for all nature and all history: the categorical enemy of production must be destroyed by one central agency of justice.[8] Consequently the youths see themselves as agents who can bring about the new social order. Mao's language in addressing the Red Guards is particularly instigating. As the youths carried out further radical actions to show their loyalty to him, he in turn made even more inciting remarks to complement their acts. This kind of communicative interaction explains the extreme harm the Red Guards inflicted on Chinese society—the interaction between demagogue and youths created a vicious cycle of incendiary discourse and motivated actions.

Roderick Hart provides an interesting vantage point from which to examine the "communication" between a demagogue and his listeners: "Most doctrines are inherently bodies of answers—they define trouble and good, prescribe courses of action, indicate ways out of trouble, and explain good options. Apparently, knowing that their listeners already 'have the answers' in the above sense, doctrinal speakers elaborate anxieties and rarely discuss solutions."[9] Mao's words are prescriptive, directing youths toward the political path he envisioned; yet it is not necessary for him to spell out how the "revolutionary action" should be implemented as he was certain the youths already had the answers he desired. Hart describes this kind of doctrinal communication as "enthymematic in that speakers can only encourage listeners to complete the speakers' reasoning."[10]

It is common for adolescents to feel self-important, egoistical, and invincible—capable of achieving anything in the world. The leadership takes advantage of youth psychology for political purposes. For example another rhetorical strategy of the Communist leadership consists of linking the self-importance of the youths to matters of national importance. By holding up a gilded image of the future, the leadership seeks to give universality and a spiritual quality of the affairs of the workaday world. Leaders convince their followers that the current times are not ordinary. The joy of belonging to the movement, the joy of being righteous in action, and ultimately the joy of victory are within the reach of all who are willing to struggle now to bring about tomorrow's utopian order.[11] Official discourse of this nature creates infinite moral reserves in youths so that revolution becomes a perpetual enterprise.

It is instructive to uncover how youths become a "rhetorical phenomenon." Michael McGee discusses how a political advocate channels and controls collective behavior: "The advocate is a 'flag-bearer' for old longings, and by transforming such longings into a new idea, he actualizes his audience's predisposition to act, thus creating a united 'people' whose collective power will warrant any reform against any other power on earth."[12] Fagen provides similar insight: "Success depends on people 'wanting' to volunteer, and it is the 'want' that becomes the object of the elite's attention and manipulation."[13] Political inculcation becomes more effective than the brute force of coercion, as the former contains complex and carefully devised stratagems. According to Kenneth Burke, "An 'ideology' is like a god coming down to earth, where it will inhabit a place pervaded by its presence. An 'ideology' is like a spirit taking up its abode in a body; it makes that body hop around in certain ways; that same body would have hopped around in different ways had a different ideology happened to inhabit it."[14] Burke's explanation suggests that the individual becomes robotic, that when he is converted to an ideology, all a political subject owns is his outer shell. His central nervous system is "remote controlled" by the demagogue. Theorists also pinpoint the infinite power of ideology and explain why an ideology can unify people with diverse values, beliefs, and interests. An ideology can even incite people to kill or to commit self-sacrifice. The Cultural Revolution provides a fitting case study.

It is not surprising then that the Red Guards, the product of official political socialization, made a complete subjective turn, radically transforming their ontological view of society. The following testimony of a Red Guard reveals the success of the change: "September 15 is a day I will never forget for the rest of my life. On this day, I became the most fortunate person in the world. Tens of thousands of words cannot describe my excited feeling. After I gave my speech, I held Chairman Mao's hand tightly. How extraordinary this pair of hands is. It was this pair of hands that liberated millions of poor people; it was this pair of hands that had been leading the Chinese revolution from one victory to another."[15]

This passage describes the inner world of a political "fanatic." The formation of this Chinese youth's political fervor did not happen overnight. He went through an extended period of a political socialization process, being continuously programmed and reprogrammed by the elite. It is fair to say the occurrence of the Chinese Cultural Revolution was largely dependent on effective political communication between the elite and the masses, and particularly the inculcation of the political fervor of the revolutionary youths. Pierre Bourdieu's critique on the symbolic power of political language sheds light on the Chinese experience: "Symbolic Power is a power that can be exercised only if it is *recognized*. What creates the power of words and slogans, a power capable of maintaining or subverting the social order, is the belief in the legitimacy of words and of those who utter them."[16]

Bourdieu illuminates the potency of political discourse; the interaction between the ideologue and his listeners becomes an ongoing and reciprocal process. When leaders churn out new party lines, the audience reacts positively because they deem them legitimate. The Chinese Cultural Revolution, which lasted for ten years with the participation of the entire nation, presents a fitting case study to support Bourdieu's claim. Linguistic unity becomes the agency with which a revolution is implemented.

On the notion of the forcefulness of a discourse community, rhetoric "permits us to create, comprehend, conserve, and criticize our worlds and ourselves. [It] accomplishes this through special attention to the situations, priorities, and strategies of actual conduct."[17] In other words *"epistemics are rhetorics are politics."*[18] In this regard rhetoric impacts or reshapes our social epistemology—how we view and comprehend the social world. Moreover rhetoric is political because it turns the possible into the transcendental.[19] While individual desires take varied forms, their basic sources are finite in their variability and widely shared. Such desires alone are not "moral"; they must be transformed by public discourse to craft a moral code. Public rhetoric can therefore be viewed as a process in which basic human desires are transformed into shared moral codes.[20] Through persuasion, individual political fervor is channeled, refashioned, and transformed into collective norms, which form the bedrock of the social order of any society. In China, through means of interactive political discourse, officially sanctioned values and beliefs become "common sense"— accepted, shared, and applied by the general public. Revolutionary norms undergird the political culture and are internalized by citizens.

How should one define the political sensibility, or rather the lack of it, among the Chinese masses during the Cultural Revolution? Thomas Hill characterizes this kind of behavior as "servile": "Servility is the absence of a certain kind of self-respect. If the effort did not require him/her to submit to humiliation or mistreatment, his/her choice would not make [him]/her servile. To defer to an expert's judgment on matters of fact is not to be servile, to defer to his every wish and whim is."[21] Servility, the absence of self-respect, manifests itself in the "irrational" behavior of the masses that become the marionettes of the ideologue. Hill's definition of servility pinpoints the cause of the Cultural Revolution.

Avishai Margalit provides another angle from which to view "respect": "There is a threshold for [the existence of respect] in people, a limit that guarantees basic respect for all human beings. The threshold that justifies respecting humans as opposed to animals is their ability to act for a reason. This threshold guarantees respect for every person capable of acting on the basis of reasons."[22] Hill's and Margalit's comments elucidate the basic trait of the Chinese people during this time period. They were servile to the official establishment because they no longer had the "ability" or "sensibility" to make sound judgments, to act on the basis of their individual rational reasoning. Their political behavior was governed by the whims of the elite.

Pan Xiao: The Introspective Generation of 1980

After the death of Mao Zedong in 1976, Deng Xiaoping, the new leader of China, introduced economic reforms. This initiative was intended not only to raise the standard of living for the Chinese but also to inaugurate a movement of new thinking suitable for an era of market economy. On December 13, 1978, Deng gave a speech titled "Liberalizing Our Thinking, Being Truthful and United to Look Ahead" at the Third Plenary Session of the Eleventh Congress of the Chinese Communist Party. Deng said, "[Our new task is to] liberalize our thinking, mobilize our brains, be truthful and unite to look ahead."[23] Deng's statement became the major party line for the era of a market economy.

Deng Xiaoping intended the Chinese people to follow a new party line that was pragmatic in theory but authoritarian in essence. Though seemingly signaling a new direction, Deng's statement is filled with contractions and incoherence. Although the reformers did not claim to be engineers of souls, they did claim responsibility, in traditional Chinese fashion, for being the guardians of souls. They feel compelled to do something to stop the perceived "unhealthy tendencies" in society. What to do, however, is inherently ambiguous. When a culture's fundamental definitions of right and wrong are in flux, there can be no uncontroversial decisions about which changes are salutary and which are unhealthy.[24] Indeed, when the era of market reform replaced the revolutionary era, political and cultural presuppositions no longer applied. Beliefs and values were in flux.

How are the Chinese people coping with the transition? Referring to it as "a journey without maps," David Apter and Tony Saich give a fitting description of the mind-set of the Chinese people during this time period: "A quite different set of possibilities becomes significant. People require new models that invoke discourse based on systematic relationships between needs, wants, priorities, preferences, and interests rather than on principles."[25] Apter and Saich describe the characteristics of a society based on economic models:

tangible practicality replaces high-sounding principles. Yet, when one political system substitutes another one, a "faultline" occurs. Since humans are thinking animals, society members will invariably search for truths so as to define and guide their actions and behavior. When truth is called into question, a crisis of faith often occurs.

Indeed, during this era, the Chinese people experience the so-called three crises of faith (*xinyang*), trust (*xinren*), and confidence (*xinxin*).[26] The crises compelled many to question their belief in Communist ideology and reevaluate their perceptions of the social reality, their political beliefs, and their self-worth. The story of Pan Xiao provides a good example of this epistemological reorientation.[27] In 1980 twenty-three-year-old Pan Xiao wrote a letter to the editor of the popular magazine *China Youth.* The letter struck such a chord with Chinese youths, attracting sixty thousand responses and sparking a nationwide discussion.[28] Titled "Why Is the Road to Life Narrower and Narrower?" Pan's letter reads: "I am twenty-three years old. I should say I have just started my life. However, I am no longer intrigued by life's secrets and attractions. I feel as if I have walked to the end of life. . . . Before, I was filled with imaginings about and longing for life. When I was in grade school, I heard stories about *How Steel Is Made* and *Lei Feng's Diary.*[29] Though I could not fully understand these stories, I was so excited upon reading them that night after night I could not fall asleep."[30] Pan went on to say how she witnessed factional fighting and property confiscations, how she was taken advantage of politically by her boyfriend, and how her best friend wrote about their private conversation in a report and handed it over to the authorities. Pan concluded, "Now Social Darwinism provides me with a deep revelation: People are selfish; there are no noble persons. The political propaganda [by the government] in the past is either fabricated or grossly exaggerated."[31]

Pan's letter should not be viewed as the venting of personal frustration and cynicism, but as representative of the feelings of many young people in her generation. With embitterment and incredulity, Pan came to realize that she had been a political dupe. Her story showcases the spiritual journey of how an ideologically driven and "hot-blooded" revolutionary youth metamorphosed into a disillusioned young adult. Values and beliefs she once held sacred turned out to be untrue and were debased. Because Communist ideals had provided her with the ultimate meaning in life, these realizations rendered her disillusionment all the more painful.[32] As Erikson has explained, "[When] the resulting self-definition, for personal or for collective reasons, becomes too difficult, *a sense of role confusion* results: The young person counterpoints—rather than synthesizes—his sexual, ethnic, occupational, and typological alternatives."[33] The term "role confusion" to a large extent explains the state of mind of Pan's generation. Apparently they are no longer the young revolutionaries who initiated change. Yet, as youths, they still feel a strong sense of responsibility. But for what cause? The higher truth they were taught to hold sacred turns out to be a sham.

The youths' cynical behavior—characterized by alienation, distrust of authority, and guilt about their gullibility—can be accompanied by deep soul-searching and reflection in order to find a new purpose to lend meaning to their lives. We find such introspection in the statements of former Red Guards, who appear to go through several stages: nostalgia, cynicism, soul searching, and ideological reorientation. These stages culminate in a subjective turn. The first stage can be described as the breaking down of their old political ideals; they discover that the political role models designated by the Communist Party were far from perfect. Chen Jiaqi, a former Red Guard, notes, "The army soldiers who participated in 'three unity' (*san jie he*) were not all as perfect as we had imagined them to be. Their rude and bullying behavior made them look like evil spirits. One really feels one's idealism is shattered."[34]

The second stage is regret-tinged nostalgia, a sentiment that has come to plague the generation who came of age during the period of political transmutation. Cai Xiang expresses their sentiment: "I pace back and forth at the crossroads, hesitant between [the camps] of collectivity and individuality. I will walk to the end of my life with a split soul that I no longer can command. I look at the star-studded sky, watching ruefully for that pair of beautiful eyes. I will never be able to walk out of the quagmire."[35]

Cai's testimony expresses the Red Guards' bewilderment over yesteryear's glory. Revolutionary times have been the best part of their lives and defined their identity. They look at that period with nostalgia, but they are no longer a part of it. Their fond memories of the revolution have been replaced by a sense of grayness. They now realize that they have at best played the role of drummer in a political farce. Cai reflects that "sacredness occupies a higher plane above us. We feel proud of it, fight for it, and cheer for it. Yet, [we also realize] it can rob cruelly the freedom and free will of an individual. Therefore, what is sacredness? In my inquisition for the past thirty years, I found out that whoever holds power is endowed with the right to define 'sacredness.'"[36]

This passage indicates the internal turmoil of Cai's generation. They came to the realization that truth is not objective but defined by those who hold power. They feel a void that nothing seems to be able to fill.[37] Now regarding themselves as "spiritual orphans,"[38] they are filled with agony because they have always taken pride in their role as the harbingers of revolution who have a "sacred" task to carry out. Yet in the end they find they have been profoundly hurt by official manipulation in the name of sacredness. Cai puts this disenchantment into perspective: "We used to fight for justice, and we used to cheer for our idealism. We were sweeping all the corners of this "sick" world. [However], we intentionally or unintentionally harmed many people, until we got hurt ourselves. No, not just hurt, our kind and beautiful aspirations had helped to destroy the greatest principle of this world—freedom."[39]

Zhu Xueqing, a former Red Guard who is now a professor at Shanghai University, provides a fitting summary of the evolving identity of the Red Guards from revolutionaries to a self-introspective group. Referring to his generation as "'68 persons" (*liuba nian ren*)—in reference to the minority of Chinese youths who engaged in independent thinking in 1968 at the height of the Cultural Revolution—he says: "The inner world of *liuba nian ren* has undergone a fission. During the Cultural Revolution, our critical-thinking ability rarely turned into our spiritual resources but rather into impulses to fight for power and a glorious life. The toxins of these two political spheres (that is, Communist culture and ideology) have seeped into our hearts."[40]

Other youths articulated in literary forms their bewilderment, disillusion, pain, and, above all, need to search for answers in a new social reality. The writings of the Obscure Poetry movement, popular in 1979–80, showcase their inner struggle. In a poem titled "One Generation," Gu Cheng wrote: "The black night has given me black eyes. / Yet, I use them to search for light."[41] Cai Kun's poem "Wrinkles" describes "Ruts left on my body, / By the reversed wheels of history."[42]

These poems vividly depict the inner world of the younger generation after the Cultural Revolution. They used poetry to articulate the confusion of having lived through a life-altering period of political upheaval. For example the pioneer of Obscure Poetry, Bei Dao, articulated the angry outcry and defiance of his generation, skillfully expressing his intense emotions about contradictions in social reality."[43] In response to the public's inability to understand Obscure Poetry, *Wenhuibao*, a major daily newspaper in Shanghai, published a commentary explaining that "to comprehend [a piece of regular writing] entails rational understanding. However, poetry expresses emotion through imagery. This way, the reader has to form the same mental picture that the poet intends him to."[44] Rather than trying to follow its logic, a reader should "feel" the poem, let the poet's emotions be in touch with the reader's intuition. From a rhetorical perspective, we can treat Obscure Poetry as the employment of metaphorical clusters to direct readers to reach the same sentiment the poet feels. Kathleen Hall Jamieson explains, "Whether or not the images or the invitation they imply are consciously intended, a rhetor's self-expressive metaphors do invite auditors to adopt their perspective. [For example], conscience is an eye; [it] is an 'eye which needs light.' An informed conscience is an eye guided by light."[45] Thus, in a rhetorical perspective, Obscure Poetry serves as an ontological guide. The poet/rhetor attempts to guide readers to reach a common consciousness.

Indeed the self-admonition of the youths is followed by an emerging political sensibility. On self-transformation, Zhu Xueqing made an apt comment: "As I believe, there are two intertwined 'Cultural Revolutions.' The first 'Cultural Revolution' is top down; the second 'Cultural Revolution' is bottom up. '68 persons may well become the backbone of the society, having experienced life at the bottom rung of the society, having learned to detect the political structure and its crevice, and having rid of the bondage of a sham ideology."[46]

The emergent political maturity manifests itself as a critique of past behavior derived from prolonged introspection. Consider Cai's new attitude toward politics: "I always regard 'sacredness' as a holy term. But now, when I apply it to social reality, I no longer impose it on you, whether I love or do not love you. Please believe me, I am no longer that thirteen-year-old boy who regards this world as sick and evil, waiting for our sweep of justice. I may not like this world, but I cannot violate it."[47]

Cai discusses what Avishai Margalit calls "self-respect" and "self-esteem," traits of politically informed citizens. According to Margalit, "Respect constitutes a ground for treating people equally, while esteem forms a basis for ranking people."[48] One can say that Chinese youths are developing their own definitions of political integrity. Their introspection, their repentance, their reinterpretation of political idealism, and their hope to mend the harm they have inflicted indicate a "subjective turn," and will pave the road for the evolution of full-blown political sensibilities in future generations.

The Outspoken Generation: The "Shekou Storm"

On January 13, 1988, the local branch of the Communist Youth League in Shekou, Guangdong Province, sponsored a symposium for seventy Shekou youths.[49] The three keynote speakers were prominent experts on youth education from the government-sponsored China Research Center for Ideological Education of Youths in Beijing. They were Li Yanjie, a professor of ethical education from Beijing Normal College; Qu Xiao, a war hero and political researcher; and Peng Qingyi, a former dancer in the Central Song and Dance Ensemble. The organizers' original intention was to invite the "experts" to deliver political talks. To their astonishment, however, the audience found the content of the talks outmoded and out of sync with a changing social reality. A heated debate ensued between the speakers and the audience about what constituted acceptable political ideals and social values in a period of market economy. At one point youths challenged Qu Xiao:

Qu Xiao: Many youths in the inland look forward to coming to the Special Economic Zone. There are two kinds of people among this group: pioneers and gold diggers.

Youth one: I hope the three teachers can have substantive discussions with us, rather than delivering empty lectures. Please explain what are gold diggers.

Youth two: Some of us come here to be contractors and to lease. Are these people gold diggers? Do the three teachers have a clear definition of what is a gold digger? To make money and to engage in the market economy are digging gold?

Qu Xiao: The gold diggers I refer to come to the Special Economic Zone for their individual interest. They are after the good life and high salaries here. I argue these people are gold diggers. One should have a noble motive and not prioritize individual interests.

Youth three: Why cannot we come to Shenzhen and Shekou to earn a living? When gold diggers make money, they have not broken the law. Though their goal is to make money, they pay taxes to the state and bring conveniences for citizens. What is wrong with being a gold digger?"[50]

The debate is evidence that the political educators and the Shekou youths live in two historical eras. The educators still have the mind-set of the revolutionary era, prioritizing politics and minimizing monetary values. To them making a sacrifice for an official cause is something that ought to be upheld. However, the mind-set of Shekou youths fits the era of market economy. To them making money through honest work is the right thing to do. To consider individual interest is not unethical. A "gold digger" should not be looked down on and in fact can be considered honorable. The incident also suggests that, at this historical juncture, the Shenzhen youths had carved out an independent identity for themselves and had engaged in their own original thinking. Their sense of right and wrong was no longer defined by official standards but by their own. The three official representatives were spokespersons of the government, promulgating official beliefs and values. The debate between them and the Shenzhen youths highlights the contrast between stalemate and progress in the market economy.

The debate, which came to be known as the Shekou Storm, attracted national attention. To print readers' reactions to it, *People's Daily* published a special column from August 8 to September 14, and received more than 1,500 letters to the editor. The writers of these letters included undergraduate and graduate students, engineers, managers, and army officers.

The Shekou debate between ideologues and youths captured what Rosen Stanley refers to as the "social mood" of China in the late 1980s, when politics, the economy, society, and ideology were all in flux.[51] In a metonymical sense, the attitude of the Shekou youths represents an emerging reconfiguration of the political sensibility of a new generation of Chinese who are emboldened, irreverent, and vocal. They demonstrate an assurance about their new role in society—a sharp contrast with the Pan Xiao generation, which was inclined to look inward. Moreover the dialogue between the demagogues and the Shekou youths suggests a changing relationship for youth and authority: a once-paternalistic, authoritarian leadership and an obedient generation of youths was transformed into a defensive, unsure authority and a new generation of youths who were inquisitive, independent, and dissatisfied with their position in society.[52] While young people were adapting their thinking to the changing environment, ideologues, personifying the Communist Party, were suspended in their outlook in the bygone revolutionary era. The debate between party educators and the Shekou youths represents the popular urge to change and the corresponding institutional effort to resist that change.

The significance of the Shekou Storm goes beyond the localized exchanges between the two camps. The youths' interaction with the party educators indicates a profound transfiguration of their political sensibility. They no longer agreed to play a role of what David Ownby terms "the 'children' to the stern, fatherly authoritative figures"[53] who have long defined the identity of the younger generation. Instead youths "strode [confidently] to the podium and delivered their own lectures as equals."[54] Ownby provides a vivid description of the placid preaching of the party educators: "The Abbies of the post-Mao era no longer had all the answers, and even if they did, post-Mao youths were not listening."[55]

Letters to the editor at the *People's Daily* reflect the public perception of the event. For example, reader Yang Fan commented that the party educators "visited many parts of the country to give speeches. Yet, they advocate a culture of 'God,' and a culture of 'role models.' They attempt to make us into one model, and convert us into [a collectivity] of one action and one ideology. Consequently [they] change the living and varied 'many' into a uniformed 'one.'"[56]

Reader Xuan Zhangnei wrote: "As I believe, the plurality of a society's values ensures its stability. It also creates the energy and creative force. In contrast, a society with a uniform set of values is only able to ensure rigidity. While the unified values may sustain the society, it suppresses the vitality and creativity of the masses."[57] One reader reacted to the Shekou Storm from another angle, saying that "an important issue arising from the Shekou Storm is the contention of two distinctively different sets of values: one that promotes the 'individual as the locus of power' (*geren benwei*), and the other 'collectivity as the locus of power' (*jiti benwei*)."[58]

Readers Yu Zhuoli and Zhang Yihui provided a fitting summary of the meaning of the Shekou Storm and the ensuing national debate: "The replacement of old values with new values cannot take place in a synchronized manner. It is a process of accumulation of quantity and a process of preparation. There is no right and wrong in the [Shekou] debate. However, everyone agrees that its significance has far exceeded the immediate circumstance."[59]

The responses of these readers reveals the pulse of the wider Chinese society in the era of economic reforms. Their letters promote the values of "plurality," "creativity," "distinctiveness," and "individuality," and the values they frown on include "stability," "rigidity," "unity," and "synchronization." The first set of values symbolizes progress and represents the new mind-set of many Chinese citizens; the second set of values represents the attitude of the government. The readers' reactions also suggest that a new generation has come into being. They are outspoken and politically sophisticated, making a huge ideological leap from the Pan Xiao generation.

In times of societal transition, the contention between the old guard and the emerging sociopolitical force centers on safeguarding or rewriting the master narrative. Indeed, in discussing a search for a master narrative for twentieth-century China, Susanne Weigelin-Schwiedrzik argues that the Chinese Communist Party dominated the interpretation of the master narrative of post-1949 Chinese political history.[60] She notes that by trying "to oblige society into accepting the idea of universal complicity," the "CCP hoped to avoid factionalism and revenge" and to "let time heal the wounds." But ongoing discussion shows that the "struggle over whose memory of the Cultural Revolution can dominate the overall assessment is gaining momentum. This struggle is not about respect but about power."[61] At the center of political and social struggle is debate over who will write the master narrative. Those who do write it will hold the power to define and interpret history. The debate between party educators and youths transcends public discussion. The old guard attempts to safeguard a master narrative that defines the moral code and norms to which they adhere. Whereas the goals of the new generation of youths are two pronged: while endeavoring to rewrite moral codes, they want to fill the role of agent of history.

The Rights Generation: Falun Gong and the Chinese People

The ontological reordering and rhetorical articulation by former Red Guards, Pan Xiao, and Shekou youths demonstrate evolution in the political sensibility of the Chinese people. They have metamorphosed from a generation of true believers to an introspective generation and then to a publicly expressive generation capable of independent thinking. The trajectory of these three generations led to the disintegration of the "closed elite political culture" (*fengbi xin zhenzhi wenhua*)—the official monopoly on ideological beliefs and values. In its place emerges a participatory political culture (*dazhong wenhua*) in which common people are making demands on the system. Yet the demands of the general population are expressed as what Kevin O'Brien and Lianjiang Li term "rightful resistance." Chinese citizens want to have "the right to have rights."[62]

How does Falun Gong fit into this picture? Unlike the forward-looking youths who are often harbingers of new social conscience, Falun Gong members are citizens from a broad range of society clamoring for basic rights. Though resistance is expressed by modern-thinking youths or by other citizens with more modest demands, one thing is certain: members of all strata of Chinese society are fighting for justice and individual rights. Nancy Chen argues that Falun Gong members are from the mainstream of Chinese society: "The organized rows of middle-aged and elderly dissenters represented a sight that was not merely disturbing for its large numbers. There were not impulsive youths as was the case a decade earlier. Instead, the protestors came from the backbone of the Chinese society."[63] The use of the term "backbone" is important. At any time period of the Chinese revolution, the people who were considered the backbone were the main force of social movement. Before 1949 they were the staunch supporters of the Chinese Communist revolution. After 1949 the government relied on these people to implement social transformation. It is not surprising that, at the height of the Falun Gong movement, when members of this backbone became supporters of Falun Gong, the government became unnerved and took reactionary measures.

The basic demand of Falun Gong believers is to exercise their rights. In a letter to the representatives of the National People's Congress, a Falun Gong member protested the official mistreatment of the group: "Now the government forbids us to speak to the degree that they fear the common people as if they were tigers (*shimin weihu*). China is so big, but there is no place for us to practice Falun Gong safely! As the highest power-holding body, the National People's Congress should certainly take into consideration the opinions of the common people. Otherwise whose will does the so-called People's Congress represent?"[64]

Members of Falun Gong express indignation about the violation of their rights. If the government claims to represent the people, they say, then it is imperative that the government must respect the will of the people. This attitude is certainly a far cry from that of the Red Guards. The political sensibility of Falun Gong is articulated as the demand to be treated with respect and justice. Citizens consider themselves to be equal to the government, which should accord them the right to have rights. A Falun Gong sympathizer offers his observation of the nature of the religious group: "It is not hard for some-one with a conscience to understand. Everyone can safeguard their opinion when it comes to the issue of right and wrong. More important, one has to understand this issue from the perspective of rights. Every Chinese has the right to choose the actions of practicing freedom of belief, rehabilitating health, performing charity, and purifying his/her mind."[65]

The author, a human-rights lawyer, notes that the key point in the con-tention between Falun Gong and the Chinese government is Falun Gong's demand for rights. They do not consider these rights to be political rights but rights based on self-respect, a new mind-set in the era of Falun Gong. Yet, as in the past revolutionary era, many citizens still consider the govern-ment as the embodiment of justice. Isabelle Thireau and Hua Linshan explain why: "The aggrieved workers sometimes also identify themselves using terms such as 'the people,' 'the workers,' or 'the masses.' Such a process can be observed in the way workers appeal to the office's officials as their protectors. Complainants often identify their interlocutors as 'uncles,' 'fair judge,' 'pro-tective god,' 'comrades,' 'directing comrades,' 'servants of the people,' and 'father and mother of the people.'"[66] The complainers, in their interaction with officials, employ an enthymeme that is rooted in a long Chinese tradi-tion: regarded as the "parents of the people," officials have the moral obliga-tion to protect the rights of their subjects and correct any wrongs. Yet the people have created a rhetorical strategy to turn the official discourse on its head: since the government holds the right to protect the people, the people have the right to ask for protection.

Falun Gong's actions are governed by "rights consciousness." In an open letter to Secretary General Kofi Annan, Falun Gong demonstrates how it is so: "Can one see any reflection of a lawful nation from the various wrongful deeds of the official suppression? Are they not trampling on the law in the capacity of law enforcers? Isn't this a serious violation of human dignity—the most basic right of a human being? People should have freedom of belief, and the freedom to express one's opinion, but we cannot have them."[67]

This passage demonstrates how basic moral codes undergird the so-called rights consciousness of Falun Gong members. They regard dignity and fair treatment as the central conditions for human existence. Let us revisit Mar-galit's claim that the overarching moral precept to guide any human society, be it democratic or authoritarian, is that it should be a "decent society"; we see that "a decent society is one whose institutions do not humiliate [their own] people. It is a decent one because people are treated with respect and honor. As a result, people in a decent society will be able to enjoy self-respect, self-esteem, integrity and dignity."[68] Margalit introduces the basic standard for a just, humane society. It is one where human dignity for all societal members is protected. Margalit's theory is thought provoking because he holds respect and dignity for citizens most sacred and reduces the political power of institutions to a secondary position. However, one must realize that the government is not the only responsible party. To maintain a "decent society," citizens must play an equally important role. While the government should not humiliate its people, people should be willing to resist if their rights are violated. In China citizens are beginning to develop the political art of recognizing humiliation, a crucial step toward being in command of their own consciences.

The growth of rights consciousness is accompanied by a subjective turn that takes the form of self-awareness—a distinct departure from the political era when the self was identified with the collectivity. For Falun Gong members, self-awareness is at first purely psychological. Members attempt to regain their self-control to cope with an adverse reality. However, the somatic self gradually gives way to a social self. It turns into a critic of the body politic. As one Falun Gong member says, "After the rule of high pressure for the past fifty years, to speak 'against one's conscience' and perform deeds 'against one's conscience' have become a norm for the Chinese. For example we have to support the slaughter at Tiananmen [in 1989] against our conscience. Amidst this, Falun Gong members stand up bravely and proudly say to the Chinese authorities: I will speak truthfully; I do not want to lie any more."[69] This passage depicts the formation of self-awareness and an independent conscience. Before the occurrence of the Falun Gong movement, the Chinese people had to commit political deeds against their consciences. Now a turning point has been reached; the Chinese stand up to the government and say with finality, "No more lies from us."

In *Weapons of the Weak*, James Scott uses the Marxist term "false consciousness" with a twist to illustrate the acquiescence of the exploited group to the rule of the state. This is made possible by the ruling class's "creating and disseminating a universe of discourse and the concepts to go with it. By defining the standards of what is true, beautiful, moral, fair, and legitimate, they build a symbolic climate that prevents subordinate classes from thinking their way free."[70] The moral discourse of Falun Gong members symbolizes the shedding of this "false consciousness" and their attempt to develop independent conscience. Or in Scott's words, the Chinese are "thinking their way free."[71]

The development of an independent conscience in turn signifies an exercise of independent judgment. Min Lin and Maria Galikowski view this as the starting point of a new epistemology. They point out: "Any universal or transcendent principles or truth should not be taken for granted and imposed on the collectivity in an arbitrary fashion." On the contrary, they say, "These truths or principles should be conceived only through individual and private comprehension, or more precisely, by means of self-recognition or through one's own personal experience."[72] Lin and Galikowski's commentary is instructive. They highlight the important quality of an "informed" citizen, who develops a more accurate perception of the social world and makes educated and informed decisions based on his or her independent judgment, free from the influence of any third party. The Chinese people have progressed through stages from rightful consciousness, to the formation of a new sensibility, and to "reprocessing" their thinking. As Chinese author Ben Xu noted, "You can search for the ultimate value from your personal experience; what you find is your own interpretation of what the ultimate value is, not the ultimate value itself; and your search is completely personal and none should monopolize the right of such a search."[73] What is implicit in his comments is that a person should exercise his own rights to search and define truth.

The events in China clearly indicate a continuing formation of a separate individual identity. However, though no longer part of the collectivity designated by the state, Chinese citizens are inclined to manifest their newly found individual identity by associating with a different kind of collectivity. The desire of the general population to participate in a collectivity is uniquely Chinese. Fayong Shi and Yongshun Cai explain: "A social network or *guanxi* contributes to co-operation among the people by promoting trust or generating moral pressure among them. Networks have a binding effect on individuals because they place much more emphasis on *renqing* (human sentiments), the long-term obligations, and bond of relationships."[74] Since antiquity the social unit rather than the individual has always been the locus of action for Chinese people. In the time of Confucius, state, clan, and family provided a man with his identity. In contemporary China the central government demands that Chinese citizens pledge their allegiance to the state—the communist collectivity. In the market economy era, collectivity, reconfigured in popular forms, continues to provide members with solidarity, a common agency to promote change. Falun Gong has consistently staged its resistance against official suppression as a "moral community." As its members perceive it, the Falun Gong community defines a common identity symbolic of morality and justice. Lin Chun argues that "individual self-realization is possible only through social empowerment; and the path to human freedom can be taken only alongside collective solidarity."[75]

The political sensibility of discontented groups also reflects a reordering of ontological perspectives. For example "contractual thinking" has come to be the ideological driving force for collective actions.[76] According to O'Brien and Li, contractual ways of thinking and a growing fluency in "rights talk" appear to underlie much of the resistance in present rural

China. Villagers are demanding fidelity to values and rights embodied in the contract-responsibility system of farming, and they are finding fault with local power holders who fail to respect the agreements.[77] Signifying the growth of the notions of "equality, rights, and rule of law,"[78] the idea of "contractual thinking" transcends the immediacy and superficiality of "rights talk." Rights have ceased to be rights to "ask for something one is entitled to" but rather rights to fulfill mutually obligatory responsibilities the government has pledged. Without their conscious knowledge, resisters have come to regard themselves as "equal" to officials in the eyes the law. To put it differently, resisters in China are demanding that the central leadership abide by the law and not "humiliate" them any more. A new sense of self-respect and dignity has enabled them to believe they have the ability to put a stop to mistreatment.

Family history offers another angle from which to view the notion of "contractual thinking." Li Changping, a county official in Hubei Province between 1983 and 2000, made an emotional appeal to the central leadership in his widely publicized book *Wo xiang zongli shuo shihua* (2002; I Told the Premier the Truth):

> My ancestors were all farmers. I have worked in the countryside for seventeen years; and I have supervised farmers for seventeen years too. [During the past seventeen years], I have witnessed the joy farmers experienced when they were given land; but I have also witnessed despair when they had to give up their land and desert their homes. [In the past seventeen years], I have also experienced too much pain: I cannot remember how many children of farmers had to give up their notice of acceptance from universities because their families could not afford to send them to school. They wept and their parents knelt down in front of me asking me for help. I cannot remember how many farmers had no place to turn to for justice, and they knelt down in front of me asking me to mete out justice for them. Issues like these are too many to name. If you come across such things once or twice, and you have not extended a helping hand, you will feel uneasy for the rest of your life. But I, in the capacity of the "official as a parent" [*fumu guan*], should have gone to hell many times in return. PLEASE TREAT PEASANTS AS CITIZENS. MAY THEY NEVER HAVE TO KNEEL DOWN AGAIN (italics added).[79]

While providing a context for understanding the mistreatment and injustice villagers have received since 1949, this firsthand account of Li Changping reflects in a compelling way the ideological leap they have made. Formerly victims of the system and occupiers of the bottom rung of the social ladders, villagers are making a demand on the system by calling for equal access to justice.

How do we define the political sensibility of the common Chinese people? Are they fighting for democracy? Are they forming a "public sphere"? Have they become politically informed citizens in the way their counterparts in liberal democratic societies have? The answer to all these questions is a definite "no." Linear Western political models neither shed light on the complexity of Chinese politics nor elucidate the torturous path on which China is progressing. As O'Brien and Li contend, resisters in China today are best thought of as "occupying a position between subjects and citizens."[80] "They risk repression at each turn, but are reasonably well positioned to 'win big' (that is, shake up power relations), provided they do not 'lose big' (that is end up being crashed by their local opponents) first."[81] Resisters in China are still parochial in their thinking. They focus on having their immediate needs met, and they place a great emphasis on how to develop winning strategies to achieve their specific goals. More often than not, the actions of the resisters are instinctual and spontaneous. They rarely reach a conceptual understanding of what their actions entail. Yet, even though they are clamoring for basic human rights, conceptually they are realizing "moral equality and self-direction"—the basis for the formation of civil and political rights, as noted by Ronald Dworkin.[82] O'Brien and Li define "citizenship" in the Chinese context: "Citizenship is not a collection of rights bestowed on passive recipients. It is an outcome of a historical process that emerges as members of the popular classes seek to improve their lot by confronting the powers-that-be. New rights are acquired only through bottom-up pressure and the painstaking extraction of concessions. Citizenship, in this sense, is less *granted* than *won*, less *accorded* than *made*."[83]

The reforms in Chinese society are likely to be a slow-motion revolution propelled by driving forces from the bottom up. Rights are likely at the top of citizens' political agenda. Rather than "a democracy without citizenship," as the official establishment would prefer it to be, Chinese style "democracy" will be one that is "fully" participatory.

When the Red Guards metamorphosed into a people with emerging political conscience, as represented by Falun Gong, their desires took a subjective turn. They are seeking equitable treatment from the government. They have come to realize that only by participating in politics fully can they achieve their goals. China will never return to the era of the Cultural Revolution, which some have rued. The Rights Revolution—a revolution of a different nature—is underway.

Implications

In recent years communication scholars have reached the consensus that Anglo-American rhetorical theory needs to undergo change. The assumption that American rhetorical theory is universally applicable should be replaced by what Dale Cyphert calls the diverse perspectives of "transcultural rhetorical theory." He notes, "As the rhetorical community grows to encompass a multicultural population, the territory of 'things incapable of being different' grows smaller and smaller, and the set of those things that are appropriately part of the rhetorical sphere seems to grow ever larger."[84] Cyphert's claim represents the growing opinion that American rhetorical theory needs a paradigm shift. Instead of centering on Anglo-American discourse, rhetorical criticism should instead include and even promote the discourses of minorities and ethnic groups such as those of African Americans or Asians.

Molefi Asante's seminal article "An Afrocentric Theory of Communication" provides an example of such views. He argues when we include the rhetoric from within an Afrocentric perspective, we develop a more complete view of the position and role of communication in the world at large. Afrocentric theory locates the study of rhetoric and communication in the heart of theoretical and philosophical debates about the nature of society.[85] The alternative discourse Raka Shome advocates is "postcolonialism," a theoretical perspective stating that modernist, neocolonial patterns of intercultural domination play a key role in reproducing the hegemony of "first world" nations. She emphasizes the "hybrid location" of cultural practices of rhetoric as a form of "border-crossing."[86] While Asante and Shome agree on the domination of Eurocentric theoretical perspectives in rhetorical criticism, they differ on how alternative perspectives should be reconfigured. Asante promotes an alternative paradigm, whereas Shome opts for a hybrid theory containing perspectives of different cultural and ethnic backgrounds. Their claims represent two approaches by communication scholars in the rearticulation of American rhetorical theory.

Intercultural scholars are also debating how to initiate reforms in Anglo-American rhetorical theory. William Starosta proposes the notion of "interacting across 'differences.'" He notes, "There is something so central to the West, the East, the national, the Buddhist" that "renders comparison cogent." The comparison "offers guidance for communication across abiding differences and styles."[87] To interact across differences will be a first step in establishing a transcultural discourse. However, differing from the early arguments of Asante and Shome, Starosta proposes what he calls "an authentic, co-equal 'third culture.'" He specifies, "Intercultural rhetoricians identify multiple ways of telling available points of view or 'narratives,' and describe who tells with what narrative and what benefit from doing so. In the end, it brings these understandings back to the intercultural interactants and dialogues."[88] Starosta suggests that the "third culture" should be a cohesive whole containing multiple theoretical perspectives occupying equal status. He elevates the position of discourse of formerly peripheral groups to equal footing with the dominant Anglo-American rhetorical theory.

If the field is increasingly ready to embrace a transcultural rhetorical theory, what form will it take? Is it to be a hodgepodge of different theoretical perspectives? Or is there a central thesis that unifies these differences? Drawing on Asante's discussion of Afrocentricity,[89] Yoshitaka Miike proposes his theory of "Asiancentricity."[90] While Asiancentricity, he notes, is about Asian shared identities and collective representations, it does not imply a desire or need to create one center in Asia. It prescribes *how* we theorize rather than *what* we theorize.[91] I endorse Miike's critical stand. By "how" we theorize, I argue, communication scholars of different cultural and ethnic backgrounds can consider how to share critical lenses and not produce rhetorical critiques that are discrete and mutually exclusive. Moreover to adopt common lenses also makes it possible for them to establish commonality across cultural boundaries.

Here cultural context occupies the center of a culturally general rhetorical criticism, no matter which culture is concerned. Transcultural scholars— Anglo-American rhetorical scholars included—converge on the perspective that culture and rhetoric are constitutive. With this stand as the major premise, rhetorical scholars of different schools conduct their specific critical inquiries, which yield distinctive data and findings. It is also plausible that the interplay of culture and rhetoric in each context assumes different forms and experiences.

The practice of regarding culture forms as frameworks for rhetorical performance aids the case study of Falun Gong. This is especially true given China's five-thousand-year history. Whether in ancient or contemporary times, culture and discourse are intertwined. Falun Gong's religious discourse is couched in cultural idioms. It upholds a moral code that is sanctioned by culture and uses classics to convey insidious messages. Culture thus provides a toolbox for promoting an alternative moral discourse. Culture also serves as a frame of reference to facilitate communication. Acculturated in a long and rich cultural tradition, the religious communications between leader and followers are enthymematic.

In its contention with Falun Gong, the Chinese government employs a formalized language to create a political campaign. Ideographs are used to evoke uniform political behavior and rally political support. These key words have historical and cultural roots in Chinese history and culture. Working together, the ideographs synchronically promote the ideology of the hegemony. A discourse community is created, and the Chinese people are united linguistically. As with the rhetoric of Falun Gong, culture undergirds the government's political communication. Rhetorical praxis in China suggests culture and rhetoric are constitutive. Culture undergirds rhetorical performances and finds expression in rhetoric. This critical stand has cultural relevance, because it could serve as a unifying concept for differences across cultural boundaries. It can also facilitate the development of a transcultural theory and commonality for scholars of diverse backgrounds.

NOTES

Prologue

1. I coined the term "New Economic Man" to contrast "New Revolutionary Man."

2. Yuqiong Zhou and Moy, "Parsing Framing Process."

3. For detailed information about the new official policy on religion, see Potter, "Belief in Control."

4. Qingjiang Yao, "China's Official Framing of Religion."

5. The religions permitted by the government include Buddhism, Taoism, Islam, and Christianity. For more details, see Potter, "Belief in Control."

6. Chiung Hwang Chen, "Framing Falun Gong."

7. Powers and Lee, "Dueling Media."

8. Lu and Simons, "Traditional Rhetoric of Chinese Communist Party Leaders."

9. Gaonkar, "The Idea of Rhetoric in the Rhetoric of Science,"

10. Campbell, "In Silence We Offend," 143.

11. Rosteck, "A Cultural Tradition in Rhetorical Studies," 229.

12. McKerrow, "Critical Rhetoric."

13. Condit, "The Character of 'History' in Rhetoric and Cultural Studies."

14. Ibid., 173–74.

15. Ibid., 174.

16. Ibid., 173.

17. Charland, "Constitutive Rhetoric."

18. Ibid., 137.

19. Ibid., 139.

20. Ibid., 142.

Chapter 1. The Rise of Falun Gong

1. In *Falun Gong's Challenge to China*, Schechter estimates Falun Gong's membership at 100 million and the membership of the Chinese Communist Party at only 56 million. Hence the number of Falun Gong practitioners would be nearly twice that of the Chinese Communist Party. The official government estimate of Falun Gong membership, however, is 2 million. In *Falun Gong in the United States*, Porter places the membership of Falun Gong in China at 7 million, noting, "With China's total urban population in 1998 at 370 million, the claim of 70 million membership would give an impossible ratio of one Falun Gong follower to every five urban Chinese. On the other hand, the 2 million figures seem far too low. A range of 2 million to 10 million practitioners is a more likely figure" (120).

2. Luo, "Yinmo zhenya falun gong de neimu."

3. Ownby, *Falun Gong and the Future of China*, 11.

4. Ownby, "A History for Falun Gong," 235.

5. Nancy Chen, "Healing Sect and Anti-Cult Campaigns," 517.

6. Ownby, *Falun Gong and the Future of China*, 88, 167.

7. Zan, "Gaige zhong de 'ruoshi qunti' de chengyin tanxi," 64.

8. Tian, "Lun dangdai shehui fenhua zhong de xinsheng ruoshi qunti," 52.

9. Zan, "Gaige zhong de 'ruoshi qunti' de chengyin tanxi," 64.

10. Tian, "Lun dangdai shehui fenhua zhong de xinsheng ruoshi qunti," 52.

11. Ibid., 52.

12. Zan, "Gaige zhong de 'ruoshi qunti' de chengyin tanxi," 64.

13. Ibid.

14. Hu Chengpeng, "Ruoshi qunti," 51–52.

15. Tian, "Lun dangdai shehui fenhua zhong de xinsheng ruoshi qunti," 52.

16. Bai, "Graduate Unemployment."

17. "Huifu gaokao sanshinian."

18. Bai, "Graduate Unemployment," 139.

19. "Daxuesheng shiye."

20. "Falii bixu zhansheng xiejiao." Government sources expressing similar views are scarce, but the government's unsympathetic attitude is best demonstrated by its failure to build a safety net.

21. Wang Sibin, "Ruoshi qunti shengcun zhuangkuang de gaishan yu shehui zhengce de tiaozheng."

22. Wang Sibin, "Shehui zhuangxing zhong de ruoshi qunti."

23. On October 23, 1985, Deng Xiaoping was interviewed by Mike Wallace for the American television program *60 Minutes*. Deng told Wallace: "We permit some people and some regions to become prosperous first, for the purpose of achieving common prosperity faster." Deng, "Shehui zhuyi he shichang jingji bu cunzai genben maodun."

24. Wang Cailing, "Baohu ruoshi qunti," 95.

25. Wang Sibin, "Ruoshi qunti shengcun zhuangkuang de gaishan yu shehui zhengce de tiaozheng."

26. Ibid., 2.

27. Solinger, "Labor Market Reform," 317.

28. Giles, Park, and Cai, "How Has Economic Restructuring Affected China's Urban Workers?," 79.

29. Ibid.

30. Ibid.

31. Chen Zhangping, ed., *Fazhan de Chuangshang*, 133.

32. Ibid., 132.

33. "Zhongguoren yali baogao."

34. "Diaocha 'laisheng shifou yuanzuo zhongguoren, wangzhan zhubian tuzao jiegu."

35. Interview with an anonymous source in Beijing, December 15, 2009.

36. Adams and Hannum, "Children's Social Welfare in China," 98.

37. Xiaoyuan Shang, Xiaoming Wu, and Yue Wu, "Welfare Provision for Vulnerable Children."

38. Ibid.

39. Wang Youqun, "Guanyu falun gong de yifengxin," 25.

40. Psychological Research Institute of the Chinese Academy of Science, *Falun Gong xianxiang de xinlixue fenxi*, 67.

41. Ibid.

42. Conversation with Lisa Weaver, Pittsburgh, February 22, 2000.

43. Zhou Yousu, "Toushi yu shenjiu," 107.

44. Ibid.

45. Ibid.

46. Nancy Chen, "Healing Sects and Anti-Cult Campaigns," 506.

47. Zhou Yousu, "Toushi yu shenjiu," 107.

48. "Falun gong jiushi xiejiao"; "Shehui de duliu"; "Huangdan de xieshuo."

49. Sara Evans first used this term in her 1979 book, *Personal Politics*.

50. Polletta, "'Free Spaces' in Collective Action," 1–2.

51. Ibid.

52. For a detailed discussion of *qigong* practice in China, see Jian Xu, "Body, Discourse, and the Cultural Politics of Contemporary Chinese Qigong."

53. Nancy Chen, *Breathing Spaces*, xi.

54. Ibid., 16.

55. Thornton, "Framing Dissent," 674.

56. Scheper-Hughes and Lock, "The Mindful Body."

57. Kleinman and Kleinman, "Somatization," 468–69.

58. Thornton, "Framing Dissect," 665.

59. Handelman, "Postlude," 247.

60. "Li Hongzhi fabiao 'wo de yidian shengming.'"

61. "Zhi lianheguo mishuzhang annan de yifeng gongkaixin."

62. O'Brien and Li, *Rightful Resistance*, 120.

63. Ibid., 2.

64. Xueguang Zhou, "Unorganized Interests," 67.

65. Li Hongzhi explains *xinxing* thus: "It includes *de*, tolerance, enlightenment quality, sacrifice, giving up ordinary people's desires and attachment, and being able to suffer hardship" (*Zhuan Falun*, 23–24).

66. Maria Hsia Chang, *Falun Gong*, 81.

67. For more discussion of scientism, see Hakfoort, "The Historiography of Scientism," and Kwok, *Scientism in Chinese Thought*, 21.

68. Johnson, "A Deadly Exercise."

69. "Muqinjie jiyu."

70. "French Police Arrest American, UK, Danish, French Citizens."

71. For example, when Sun Jiazheng, the Chinese minister of culture, visited France, Falun Gong practitioners sued him in a Paris court for torturing Falun Gong members in China. See Smith, "Sect Sues Minister."

72. Yuezhi Zhao, "Falun Gong, Identity, and the Struggle over Meaning Inside and Outside China," 217.

73. O'Brien and Li, *Rightful Resistance*, 71.

74. Bowers, Ochs, and Jensen, *The Rhetoric of Agitation and Control*, 36–43.

75. This term is used in contrast to "out of order," which is discussed extensively in Wilkinson, "The Rhetorical Analysis of Movements."

76. Jiang, "Speech to Commemorate the Founding."

77. For further information on the growth of the political sensibility of the Chinese, see, for example, Hook, ed., *The Individual and the State in China*, and Weston and Jensen, eds., *China beyond the Headlines*.

78. Bakken, *The Exemplary Society*, 21.

79. Goldman and MacFarquhar, eds., *The Paradox of China's Post-Mao Reforms*, 16.

80. Johnson, *Wild Grass*, 7.

81. Tocqueville, *The Old Régime*, 176–77.

82. Pei, *From Reform to Revolution*, 45.

83. Bakken, *The Exemplary Society*, 26.

84. Ibid., 26–27.

85. Mannheim, *Ideology and Utopia*, 218.

86. "Chongfen renshi falun gong zuzhi de zhengzhi benzhi."

87. "Yifa zhiguo, yancheng xiejiao."

88. Yasuo Onishi, *Epilogue*.

89. "Three Represents" refers to the way in which the Chinese Communist Party represents the development of an advanced productive force, the direction of the advanced Chinese culture, and the basic interest of the Chinese people.

90. Ewing, "Hu Jintao."

91. "Hu Delivers New Year's Message."

92. Ren Buxou, "Hu Jintao shidai de xinling saodong."

93. Ibid.

94. Ibid.

95. "Yiren weiben, guanzhu anquan, guan ai sheng ming," 1.

96. "Full Text of Premier Wen's Speech at Harvard."

97. Wenfang Tang, *Public Opinion and Political Change in China*, 196.

98. Ibid., 122.

99. "Zhongguo wangzhan mianlin dengji 'weiji.'"

100. Ibid.

101. *China News Digest.*

102. Li Weixing, "Bugei cuowu sixiang tigong chuanbo qudao."

103. "Bawo yulun daoxiang, zengqiang yindao yulun de benling."

104. Ozouf, "'Public Opinion' at the End of the Old Regime," S1.

105. Quoted in ibid., S3.

106. Ibid., S9.

107. Wenfang Tang, *Public Opinion and Political Change in China*, 23.

108. Weaver, *The Ethics of Rhetoric*, 211.

109. Chen Jiaxing, "Shuoshuo 'yiren weiben.'"

110. "Qinmin aimin zhengfu xingxiang."

111. Ibid.

112. Ibid.

Chapter 2. Challenging Contemporary Political Culture

1. James W. Jones, *Contemporary Psychoanalysis*, 14.

2. I coined the term "New Communist Man" after reading Richard Fagen's *Transformation of Political Culture in Cuba*. Fagen proposed the term "New Revolutionary

Man." I was inspired by his use of the term, as it best captures the spirit of a reformed revolutionary.

3. I borrowed this term from Maurice Charland's "Constitutive Rhetoric" for use in reference to the "unindoctrinated."

4. In his *Communist Manifesto*, Marx argued that history involves a continual class struggle based on "economic determinism." His theory holds that the laboring class (the proletariat) undermines the power of capitalists and will eventually establish a new system, which we call "communism" and which communists call "socialism." Lenin expanded on Marx's ideas of the dictatorship of the proletariat. His main thesis was that communists should take steps to bring about the overthrow of the capitalist system. For this, communists needed to organize a tightly controlled, disciplined party ready for violent revolution. See Yoder, *Communism in Transition*, 8–9.

5. Kwok, *Scientism in Chinese Thought*, 24.

6. Mao, "Shijianlun," 1:259–60.

7. MacInnis, *Religion in China Today*, 32–33.

8. Wang Meng, "Renwen jingshen wenti yougan," 109.

9. For detailed discussions on how the conflict between Falun Gong and Chinese central leadership started, see Fu, *Kexue zhi jian*.

10. Zhu Xi (1130–1200) and Cheng Yi (1033–1108) were proponents of Neo-Confucianism—a revival of Confucianism that became dominant during the Song (960–979) and Ming (1368–1643) dynasties. Zhu and Cheng promoted adherence to social hierarchies, advocating in particular the belief that a man should overcome "human desire" to reach enlightenment. The phrase "to kill with ethics" refers to the rigid code of ethics upheld by Zhu and Cheng.

11. He Zuoxiu, *Wo bu xinxie*, 23–25.

12. Aune, *Rhetoric and Marxism*, 112.

13. He Zuoxiu, *Wo bu xinxie*, 171.

14. Aune, *Rhetoric and Marxism*, 143.

15. He Zuoxiu, *Wo bu xinxie*, 294.

16. Aune, *Rhetoric and Marxism*, 144–45.

17. Apter and Saich, *Revolutionary Discourse*, 6.

18. Ibid.

19. Aune, *Rhetoric and Marxism*, 143.

20. Tsou, *The Cultural Revolution and Post-Mao Reforms*, 4.

21. Apter and Saich, *Revolutionary Discourse*, 21.

22. Ibid., 267.

23. Uhalley, *A History of the Chinese Communist Party*, 58.

24. Apter and Saich, *Revolutionary Discourse*, 6

25. Ibid., 26.

26. Ibid., 268.

27. Ibid.

28. Li Rui, *Zhiyan*, 43. Li is currently a member of the Central Advisory Committee of the Chinese Communist Party.

29. Ibid., 44.

30. Ibid.

31. Mao, "Oppose Stereotyped Party Writing," 509.

32. Mao, "Talks at the Yenan Forum," 3: 877–78.

33. Grieder, *Intellectuals and the State in Modern China*, x.

34. Jonathan Spence, *The Gate of Heavenly Peace*, xv.

35. Liu Shaoqi, "How to Be a Good Communist," 108.

36. Mao, "Talks at the Yenan Forum," 3:808.

37. Fagen, *The Transformation of Political Culture in Cuba*.

38. Mao, "Rectify the Party's Style of Work," 3:779–80.

39. Liu Shaoqi, "How to Be a Good Communist," 136–37.

40. Apter and Saich, *Revolutionary Discourse*, 179.

41. McGee, "In Search of the 'People,'" 346.

42. Apter and Saich, *Revolutionary Discourse*, 155–56.

43. Ibid.,141.

44. Wang Jiaxiang (1906–1974) was appointed the deputy head of the study group of Central Committee of Chinese Communist Party in the Yenan campaign and was directly involved in leading it. In his 1947 speech "The Road to Liberation of the Chinese Communist Party and Chinese People," he first proposed the term "Mao Zedong Thought." See Hu Sheng, ed., *The Seventy Years of the Chinese Communist Party*, 202.

45. Li Rui, *Zhiyan*, 312.

46. Hu Sheng, ed., *The Seventy-Year History of the Chinese Communist Party*, 202.

47. Ibid., 202.

48. Xu Liangying, *Science and Socialist Construction in China*, 211.

49. Quoted in Shiping Hua, *Scientism and Humanism*, 68.

50. Kwok, *Scientism in Chinese Thought*, 21.

51. Ibid., 200.

52. Sorell, *Scientism*, 1.

53. Taylor, *Defining Science*, 5.

54. Weaver, *The Ethics of Rhetoric*, 215.

55. Rothbard, "The Mantle of Science," 165.

56. Wei Chengsi, ed., *Zhongguo dangdai kexue sichao*, 557.

57. Ibid., 598.

58. "Jianchi congyan zhidang."

59. "Yingzao wenming kexue de shehui huanjing."

60. Kwok, *Scientism in Chinese Thought*, 53.

61. Brooke, *Science and Religion*, 337.

62. Young, *Totalitarian Language*, 137.

63. Bakken, *The Exemplary Society*, 53.

64. "Falii bixu zhansheng xiejiao."

65. Li Hongzhi, *Zhuan Falun*, 2.

66. Shang Jiuyun, "Shilun zhongjiao zhi gongneng," 54.

Chapter 3. Why Is Falun Gong Popular?

1. Ben Xu, *Disenchanted Democracy*, 10.

2. Ibid., 5.

3. Yurchak, *Everything Was Forever*, 2.

4. Blumenberg, *Work on Myth*, 7.

5. Roof, *Spiritual Marketplace*, 9

6. Giddens, *Modernity and Self-Identity*, 53.

7. Apter and Saich, *Revolutionary Discourse*, 5.

8. Ibid., 320.

9. Ibid., 321.

10. Lin and Galikowski, *The Search for Modernity*, 23.

11. Li Yixiang, "Yige boshisheng yu falun gong de juelie."

12. Publisher's comment on back cover of Kleinman, Das, and Lock, eds., *Social Suffering*.

13. Lyon and Barbalet, "Society's Body," 50.

14. Csordas, "The Body as Representation."

15. James W. Jones, *Contemporary Psychoanalysis*, 31.

16. Ibid., 14.

17. Zhao Yangong, "Hepin jiejue falun gong wenti."

18. Li Hongzhi, *Zhuan Falun*, 3.

19. Fung Yu-Lan (Feng Youlan), *A History of Chinese Philosophy*, 237.

20. Li Hongzhi, *Zhuan Falun*, 128.

21. Maria Hsia Chang, *Falun Gong*, 76.

22. Li Hongzhi, *Zhuan Falun*, 148–49.

23. Li refers to formal codes of behaviors that define traditional interpersonal relationships. They are commonly translated as "rites," "propriety," and "decorum."

24. Li Hongzhi, *Zhuan Falun*, 5.

25. Ibid., 140.

26. Gould, *The Ancient Quarrel Between Poetry and Philosophy*, ix.

27. Morris, "About Suffering, 41.

28. Li Hongzhi, *Zhuan Falun*, 324.

29. Morris, "About Suffering."

30. Shi, "Ni xingfu ma?"

31. Zhou Yousu, "Toushi yu shenjiu," 105.

32. Wang Youqun, "Guanyu falun gong de yifengxin," 26.

33. Ibid.

34. James, *Writings*, 79–81.

35. Shulman and Stroumsa, "Persons, Passages and Shifting Cultural Space."

36. Chuang Tzu, *Basic Writings*, 29.

37. Ibid.,100–101.

38. Chen Jiqun, "Falun dafa jinghuale wode shenti, chunjiele wode xinling," 3.

39. Geertz, *The Interpretation of Cultures*, 127.

40. Hsu, "The Self in Cross-Cultural Perspective."

41. Hu Ping, "Cong falun gong xianxiang tanqi (shang)."

42. Giddens, *Modernity and Self-Identity*, 51.

43. Handelman, "Postlude," 240.

44. Shang Jiuyun, "Shilun zongjiao zhi gongneng."

45. Shulman and Stroumsa, "Persons, Passages and Shifting Cultural Space," 4.

46. I am aware that, since the time of Sigmund Freud, there have been different opinions about this categorization in contemporary Western philosophy. Here I refer to the popular perception regarding the dichotomy of mind and body. This is especially true in Western medicine, which rarely links physical symptoms with mental perception in a biomedical perspective.

47. Deutsch, "The Concept of Body," 6.

48. Ames, "The Meaning of Body," 164–65.

49. Ibid.,160.

50. Ibid.

51. Boodberg, "Introduction to Fung Yulan's History of Chinese Philosophy."

52. Ames, "The Meaning of Body," 167.

53. *Kuan Tzu*, 16.4a–b.

54. Ames, "The Meaning of Body," 167–68.

55. *Kuan Tzu*, 16.4a.

56. In ancient Greek cosmology, one finds a parallel to the Chinese classical notion that heaven, earth, mind, and body all maintain positive relationships. According to Greek beliefs, gods and humans existed together within the same universal order and were ruled by the same moral laws; yet the separation between them was unbridgeable. See Padel, *In and Out of the Mind*.

57. Ames, "The Meaning of Body," 166.

58. Hahn, *Sickness and Healing*, 77.

59. Kleinman, *Patients and Healers*, 163.

60. Hahn, *Sickness and Healing*, 78.

61. Ibid.

62. Ibid.

63. Ibid.

64. Kleinman, *Patients and Healers*, 263–64.

65. Ibid., 264.

66. Li Hongzhi, *Zhuan Falun*, 2.

67. Kleinman, *Patients and Healers*, 367.

68. Ibid., 360.

69. Ibid.

70. Haraway, *Simians, Cyborgs, and Women*, 191, 198.

71. Csordas, "The Body as Representation," 5.

72. Nancy Chen, *Breathing Spaces*, 16.

73. Handelman, "Postlude," 236–253.

74. Wander, "The Third Persona," 376.

75. Roof, *Spiritual Marketplace*, 169.

76. Ibid., 170.

77. Witten, *All Is Forgiven*, 29.

78. Handelman, "Postlude," 240.

Chapter 4. As Powerful as Weapons

1. A "rhetorical situation" is defined as one in which a rhetor uses available means to sway an audience's opinion. See Bitzer, "The Rhetorical Situation."

2. Hayden White, *Tropics of Discourse*, 91.

3. Charles B. Jones, "Transitions in the Practice and Defense of Chinese Pure Land Buddhism."

4. Dillistone, "The Relationship between Form and Content," 124–25.

5. According to Ann Swidler, "culture" can work as "a 'toolkit' of symbols, stories, rituals, and worldviews, which people may use in varying configurations to solve different kinds of problems" (Swidler, "Culture in Action," 273).

6. Ge Gao and Xiaosui Xiao, "Intercultural/Interpersonal Research," 26.

7. Xing Lu, "Chinese Political Communication," 108.

8. Yingqin Liu, "Cultural Factors and Rhetorical Patterns," 197.

9. See for example Ge Gao and Xiaosui Xiao, "Intercultural/Interpersonal Communication Research."

10. Gudykunst and Ting-Toomey, *Culture and Interpersonal Communication*, 100.

11. Brown, *Transfiguration*, 3.

12. Ibid., 15.

13. Franke, "Metaphor and the Making of Sense," 148–49.

14. Li Hongzhi, *Zhuan Falun*, 164–65.

15. Shek, "The Alternative Moral Universe," 47.

16. Franke, "Metaphor and the Making of Sense," 148–49.

17. Miller, "Seeing Through a Glass Darkly," 221.

18. Li Hongzhi, *Zhuan Falun*, 23.

19. Schoenhals, *Doing Things with Words*, 3.

20. My comments on Li Hongzhi's use of simile as a rhetorical device are inspired by John Dixon's statement on simile in Christian art. I see a parallel because both contain qualities that rouse believers to action. See Dixon, "The Way into Matter."

21. Li Hongzhi, *Falun fofa*, 26.

22. Li Hongzhi, *Zhuan Falun*, 3.

23. Waddell and Dillistone, introduction to *Art and Religion as Communication*, 11.

24. Li Hongzhi, *Zhuan Falun*.

25. Lakoff and Johnson, *Metaphors We Live By*, 25.

26. Li Hongzhi, *Zhuan Falun*, 323.

27. Lakoff and Johnson, *Metaphors We Live By*, 26.

28. Whitehill, "The Indirect Communication."

29. Ibid., 85.

30. James W. Jones, *Contemporary Psychoanalysis*, 40.

31. Whitehill, "The Indirect Communication," 93.

32. Ibid., 91.

33. Li Hongzhi, *Zhuan Falun*, 111–12.

34. Markus, Crane, Bernstein, and Siladi, "Self-Schemas and Gender."

35. Mao Zedong first used the term "sugar-coated bullet" at the Second Plenary Meeting of the Seventh Central Committee on March 5, 1949. On the eve of the Chinese Communist Party takeover in China, Mao warned party members to watch out for attacks from opposing parties, which would assume more subterranean forms. See Mao, "The Report at the Second Plenary Meeting," 4:1314–29.

36. "Shehui de duliu, renmin de huohai."

37. Gao Gao and Yan Jiaqi, *Wenge shinianshi*, 2.

38. "Bixu qizhi xianming di fandui dongluan."

39. Hayden White, *Tropics in Discourse*, 109.

40. "Jiepi Li Hongzhi jiqi 'Falun dafa' shi yichang yansu de zhengzhi douzheng."

41. Chiung Hwang Chen, "Framing Falun Gong," 27.

42. Powers and Lee, "Dueling Media," 268.

43. For more discussion of the rhetorical strategy of polarization employed by the Chinese Communist Party in political campaigns, see Hu Sheng, ed., *The Seventy-Year*

History of the Chinese Communist Party; Hu Ping, Chanji; Gao Gao and Yan Jiaqi, Wenge shinianshi; Winston L. Y. Yang and Marshal L. Wagner, eds., *Tiananmen.*

44. "Falii bixu zhansheng xiejiao."

45. Ownby, *Falun Gong and the Future of China,* 180.

46. Powers and Lee, "Dueling Media," 271.

47. "Quanguo gedi ganbu qunchong biaoshi jianjue yonghu dang he zhengfu chuli falun gong wenti de jueding."

48. Wasburn, *Broadcasting Propaganda,* 57.

49. "Yingzao wenming kexue de shehui huanjing."

50. Liu Guanjun, "Lun Jiang Zemin bianzheng weiwu zhuyi kexue jishuguan de neihan," 10.

51. Liu Xiaoting, "Dui kexue yu zongjiao huanxi guanxi de zhishi shehui fenxi," 45.

Chapter 5. "Wildfire won't wipe it out—Spring wind blows it back"

1. The lines quoted in the chapter title are from "Fu de guyuancao songbie" [A Poem of Farewell on the Grass of Ancient Plain] by Tang poet Bai Juyi (772–846), quoted from Department of Chinese Language, Wuhan University, ed., *Sanbanshou xinxuan tangshi,* 322. Swidler, "Culture in Action," 279.

2. Gao Gao and Yan Jiaqi, *Wenge shinianshi,* 51.

3. Ibid., 41.

4. Fagen, *The Transformation of Political Culture in Cuba,* 16–17.

5. Erikson, *Identity,* 89.

6. Ibid.

7. Gao Gao and Yan Jiaqi, *Wenge shinianshi,* 43.

8. Erikson, *Identity,* 84.

9. Hart, "The Rhetoric of the True Believer," 252.

10. Ibid., 251.

11. Fagen, *Transformation,* 12.

12. McGee, "In Search of 'the People,'" 344–45.

13. Fagen, 10.

14. Burke, *Language as Symbolic Action,* 6.

15. Jiang Pei, ed., *Laoxinwen,* 52–53.

16. Bourdieu, *Language and Symbolic Power,* 170.

17. Nelson, "Political Foundations for the Rhetoric of Inquiry," 267.

18. Ibid., 268.

19. Ibid.

20. Condit, "Crafting Virtue," 310–11.

21. Hill, *Autonomy and Self-Respect,* 6.

22. Margalit, *The Decent Society,* 65.

23. Deng, "Jiefang sixiang, shishiqiushi, tuanjie yizhi xiangqiankan," 140.

24. Madsen, "The Spiritual Crisis of China's Intellectuals," 244.

25. Apter and Saich, *Revolutionary Discourse,* 320. Apter and Saich use the terms "symbolic capital" and "logocentric model" interchangeably to draw a contrast to the ecocentric model.

26. Luo Xu, *Searching for Life's Meaning,* 68.

27. Pan Xiao is the pen name of two women, Pan Yi and Huang Xiaoju.

28. Luo Xu, *Searching for Life's Meaning,* 57.

29. How Steel is Made is a novel about a Red Army soldier, who, despite unimaginable hardships and adversity, remains steadfast to the communist cause. The novel was popular in China during the 1950s and 1960s.

30. Pan, "Why Is the Road to Life Narrower and Narrower?" (letter to the editor), 3.

31. Ibid., 8–9.

32. Ownby, "The Audience," 227.

33. Erikson, *Identity*, 87.

34. Chen Jiaqing, "Zhizhuo yu mimang," 319.

35. Cai, "Shensheng huiyi," 265.

36. Ibid., 262–63.

37. Chen Jiaqing, "Zhizhuo yu mimang," 317.

38. Hu Fayun, "Hong luyi," 214.

39. Cai, "Shensheng huiyi," 262.

40. Zhu Xueqing, "Sixiangshi shang de shizongzhe," 333.

41. Tay, "'Obscure Poetry,'" 143.

42. Ibid.

43. Yu Zhuoli and Zhang Yijui, *Muji*, 58.

44. Ibid.

45. Jamieson, "The Metaphoric Cluster," 60, 72.

46. Zhu Xueqing, "Sixiangshi shang de shizongzhe," 333.

47. Cai, "Shensheng huiyi," 261.

48. Margalit, *Decent Society*, 44.

49. Shekou is an industrialized district in the Shenzhen Special Economic Zone (SEZ) in Guangdong Province. In 1988 there were about twenty-six thousand employees working in the district, and about 80 percent of them were young adults. Because Shenzhen was among the first Chinese coastal cities to open up to the world, it continued to attract a large number of young people who wanted to pursue their "Chinese Dream."

50. "1988 nian de Shekou Fengbo."

51. Rosen, "Youth and Social Change in the PRC," 289.

52. Ownby, "The Audience," 215.

53. Ownby, "The Audience," 217.

54. Ibid., 244.

55. Ibid., 223.

56. Yang Fan, "Shekou fengbo de qianqian houhou."

57. Xuan, "Duoyangxing caineng baozheng wending he huoli."

58. Yang Fan, "'Shekou Fengbo.'"

59. Yu Zhuoli and Zhang Yijui, *Muji*, 219.

60. Weigelin-Schwiedrzik, "In Search of a Master Narrative," 1071.

61. Ibid., 1091.

62. O'Brien and Li, *Rightful Resistance*, 119.

63. Nancy Chen, "Healing Sects and Anti-Cult Campaigns," 514.

64. "Zhi quanguo renda daibiao de yifeng gong kaixin."

65. Ye, "Falun gong yi liangzhi huanxing zhonghuaminzu."

66. Thireau and Linshan, "The Moral Universe of Aggrieved Chinese Workers."

67. "Zhi lianheguo mishuzhang annan de yifeng gongkaixin."

68. Margalit, *The Decent Society*, 1.

69. Xiao Xiaojun, "Buzai weixin."

70. Scott, *Weapons of the Weak*, 39–40.

71. Ibid., 40.

72. Lin and Galikowski, *The Search for Modernity*, 193.

73. Ben Xu, *Disenchanted Democracy*, 51–52.

74. Shi and Cai, "Disaggregating the State," 315.

75. Lin, *The Transformation of Chinese Socialism*, 227.

76. For detailed discussions on "contractual thinking," see for example Baogang He, "Village Citizenship in China; Liebman, "Watchdogs or Demagogues?"; O'Brien, "Neither Transgressive nor Contained."

77. O'Brien and Li, *Rightful Resistance*, 7

78. Ibid., 4.

79. Li Changping, *Wo xiang zongli shuo shihua*, 6–7.

80. O'Brien and Li, *Rightful Resistance*, 120.

81. Ibid., 123.

82. Dworkin, "Taking Rights Seriously in Beijing."

83. O'Brien and Li, *Rightful Resistance*, 119–120.

84. Cyphert, "Ideology, Knowledge and Text," 385.

85. Asante, "An Afrocentric Communication Theory." 552–62.

86. Shome, "Postcolonial Interventions in the Rhetorical Canon."

87. William Starosta, "Rhetoric and Culture," 67.

88. Ibid., 65–67.

89. Asante, "Communicating Africa."

90. Miike defines "Asiancentricity" as "an assertation of Asians as subjects and agents; the centrality of the collective and humanistic interests of Asia and Asians in the knowledge reconstruction about the Asian world, and the placement of Asian cultural values and ideals at the center of inquiry into Asian thought and action." See Miike, "An Anatomy of Eurocentrism."

91. Ibid., 4.

BIBLIOGRAPHY

Adams, Ian, Riley Adams, and Rocco Galati. *Power of the Wheel: The Falun Gong Revolution*. Toronto: Stoddart, 2000.

Adams, Jennifer, and Emily Hannum. "Children's Social Welfare in China, 1989–1997: Access to Health Insurance and Education." *China Quarterly* 181 (March 2005): 98–136.

"All Set for 16th CPC National Congress: Spokesman." Online at *Chinadaily.com.cn*. http://app1.chinadaily.com.cn/highlights/party16/news/1107all.html (accessed January 12, 2005).

Ames, Roger T. "The Meaning of Body in Classical Chinese Philosophy." In *Self as Body in Asian Theory and Practice*, edited by Thomas Kasulis with Roger T. Ames and William Dissanayake, 157–77. Albany: State University of New York Press, 1993.

Apter, David E., and Tony Saich. *Revolutionary Discourse in Mao's Republic*. Cambridge, Mass.: Harvard University Press, 1994.

Asante, Molefi. "An Afrocentric Communication Theory." In *Contemporary Rhetorical Theory: A Reader*, edited by John Louis Lucaites, Celeste Michelle Condit, and Sally Caudit, 552–62. New York: Guildford Press, 1999.

———. "Communicating Africa: Enabling Centricity for Intercultural Engagement." *China Media Research* 3, no. 3 (2007): 70–75.

Aune, James. *Rhetoric and Marxism*. Boulder, Colo.: Westview, 1994.

Austin, J. L. *How to Do Things with Words*. London: Oxford University Press, 1962.

Bai, Limin, "Graduate Unemployment: Dilemmas and Challenges in China's Move to Mass Higher Education." *China Quarterly* 185 (March 2006): 128–44.

Bakken, Børge. *The Exemplary Society: Human Improvement, Social Control, and the Dangers of Modernity in China*. New York: Oxford University Press, 1999.

Bao Guizhen, and Zou Qian. "Jidujiao yu fojiao lunli sixiang bijiao yanjiu" [A Comparative Study in the Ethical Thought of Christianity and Buddhism]. *Xibei minzu xueyuan xuebao* [Academic Journal of Northeastern Academy of Minority Nationalities], no. 3 (2002): 33–37.

"Bawo yulun daoxiang, zengqiang yindao yulun de benling" [Direct Public Opinion and Develop Our Ability to Channel Public Opinion]. Online at http://www.people.com.cn/GB/shizheng/1026/3054959.html (accessed July 16, 2010).

Bell, Daniel. *Beyond Liberal Democracy: Political Thinking for an East Asian Context* Princeton: Princeton University Press, 2006.

Berger, Peter. *The Sacred Canopy: Elements of a Sociological Theory of Religion*. Garden City, N.Y.: Doubleday, 1967.

———. *The Syncretic Religion of Lin Chao-en.* New York: Columbia University Press, 1980.

Bitzer, Lloyd. "The Rhetorical Situation." In *Contemporary Rhetorical Theory: A Reader,* edited by John Louis Lucaites, Celeste Michelle Condit, and Sally Caudit, 217–25. New York: Guildford Press, 1999.

"Bixu qizhi xianming di fandui dongluan" [We Must Take a Clear-Cut Stand against Disturbances]. *People's Daily,* overseas edition, April 6, 1989.

Black, Edwin. *Rhetorical Criticism: A Study in Method.* New York: Macmillan, 1965.

Bloom, Gerald, and Shenglan Tang, eds. *Healthcare Transition in Urban China.* Aldershot: Ashgate, 2004.

Blumenberg, Hans. *Work on Myth.* Translated by Robert M. Wallace. Cambridge, Mass.: MIT Press, 1985.

Bobbit, David, and Harold Mixon. "Prophecy and Apocalypse in the Rhetoric of Martin Luther King, Jr." *Journal of Communication and Religion* 17 (March 1994): 27–38.

Bodde, Derk. *Essays on Chinese Civilization.* Edited by Charles Le Blanc and Dorothy Borei. Princeton: Princeton University Press, 1981.

Boodberg, Peter. "Introduction to Fung Yulan's History of Chinese Philosophy." *Far Eastern Quarterly* 13 (1954): 334–37.

Bormann, Ernest G. "Fantasy and Rhetorical Vision: The Rhetorical Criticism of Social Reality." *Quarterly Journal of Speech* 58, no. 4 (1972): 396–407.

Bourdieu, Pierre. *Language and Symbolic Power.* Cambridge, Mass.: Harvard University Press, 1994.

Bowers, John, Donovan Ochs, and Richard Jensen. *The Rhetoric of Agitation and Control.* Prospect Heights, Ill.: Waveland Press, 1993.

Brooke, John H. *Science and Religion: Some Historical Perspectives.* New York: Cambridge University Press, 1991.

Brown, Frank B. *Transfiguration: Poetic Metaphor and the Languages of Religious Belief.* Chapel Hill: University of North Carolina Press, 1983.

Burke, Kenneth. *Language as Symbolic Action: Essays on Life, Literature, and Method.* Berkeley: University of California Press, 1966.

Cai Xiang. "Shensheng huiyi" [Sacred Memories]. In *1966: women nayidai de huiyi* [1966: Recollections of Our Generation], edited by Xu Youyu, 253–65. Beijing: Zhongguo wenlian chubanshe, 1998.

Campbell, Karlyn Kohrs. "In Silence We Offend." In *Toward the Twenty-First Century: The Future of Speech Communication,* edited by Julia Wood and Richard Gregg, 137–50. Cresskill, N.J.: Hampton Press, 1995.

Cao Jingqing, ed. *Ruxue fuxing zhilu: Liao Shuming wenxuan* [The Confucian Road of Restoration: The Selected Works of Liang Shuming]. Shanghai: Yuandong chubanshe, 1994.

Chan, Adrian. *Chinese Marxism.* London: Continuum, 2003.

Chan, Wing-Tsit. *A Source Book in Chinese Philosophy.* Princeton: Princeton University Press, 1963.

Chang, Maria Hsia. *Falun Gong: The End of Days.* New Haven: Yale University Press, 2004.

Chang Wei and Luo Yi. *Guomin xintai fangtan* [Visiting and Learning the Mental State of Chinese Citizens]. Beijing: Zhongguo wuzi chubanshe, 1998.

Charland, Maurice. "Constitutive Rhetoric: The Case of the *Peuple québécois.*" *Quarterly Journal of Speech* 73, no. 2 (1987): 133–50.

Chen, Chiung Hwang. "Framing Falun Gong: Xinhua News Agency's Coverage of the New Religious Movement in China. *Asian Journal of Communication,* 15, no. 1 (2005): 16–36.

Chen, Jie, and Peng Deng. *China since the Cultural Revolution: From Totalitarianism to Authoritarianism.* Westport, Conn.: Praeger, 1995.

Chen, Nancy. *Breathing Spaces: Qigong, Psychiatry, and Healing in China.* New York: Columbia University Press, 2003.

———. "Healing Sects and Anti-Cult Campaigns." *China Quarterly* 174 (2003): 505–20.

Chen Aimei and Xu Xiaohui. "Zhongguo shehui zhuanxingqi xiandaihua fansi" [Reflection on the Modernization of Chinese Society in a Transitional Period]. *Changchun shifan xueyuan xuebao* [Changchun Normal College Academic Journal] 21 (2002): 8–11.

Chen Chen. "Wo ceng zuo zai lun yi shang" [I Used to Sit in a Wheel Chair]. *Qingliu* (Falun Gong publication) no.12 (2003): 5.

Chen Jiaqing. "Zhizhuo yu mimang" [Devotion and Loss]. In *1966: women nayidai de huiyi* [1966: Recollections of Our Generation], edited by Xu Youyu, 307–19. Beijing: Zhongguo wenlian chubanshe, 1998.

Chen Jiaxing. "Shuoshuo 'yiren weiben'" [On "People as Essence"]. Online at http://www.people.com.cn/GB/guandian/1033/2376272.html (accessed June 15, 2005)

Chen Jiqun. "Falun dafa jinghuale wode shenti, chunjiele wode xinling" [Falun Gong Has Purified My Body and Cleansed My Soul]. *Falun dafa* (Falun Gong publication), no.7 (2000).

Chen Peihua. *Maozhuxi de haizimen: hongweibing yidai de chengzhang he jingli* [The Children of Chairman Mao: The Development and Experience of the Red Guard Generation]. Taipei: Gongguan tushu, 1997.

Chen Zhangping, ed. *Fazhan de Chuangshang: Chengdushi xiagang nugong xianzhuang baogao* [The Wound of Development: A Report on the Livelihood of the Laid-Off Female Worker in Chengdu City]. Chengdu: Sichuan People's Publishing House, 2001.

Chin, Andrew. *Chinese Humanism: A Religion beyond Religion.* Taipei: Fu Jen Catholic University Press, 1981.

China News Digest. Online at http://my.cnd.org/modules/news/print.php?storyid=7203 (accessed July 26, 2010).

"Chongfen renshi falun gong zuzhi de zhengzhi benzhi" [Fully Realize the Political Nature of Falun Gong]. *People's Daily,* overseas edition, March 8, 1999.

Chuang Tzu. *Basic Writings.* Translated by Burton Watson. New York: Columbia University Press, 1964.

Cohen, Jean L., and Andrew Arato. *Social Movement and Civil Society.* Cambridge, Mass.: MIT Press, 1992.

Condit, Celeste Michelle. "The Character of 'History' in Rhetorical Cultural Studies: Recording Genetics." In *At the Intersection: Cultural Studies and Rhetorical Studies,* edited by Thomas Rosteck, 168–85. New York: Guildford Press, 1999.

———. "Crafting Virtue: The Rhetorical Construction of Public Morality." In *Contemporary Rhetorical Theory: A Reader,* edited by John Louis Lucaites, Condit, and Sally Caudill, 306–25. New York: Guilford Press, 1999.

Confucius. *The Analects*. Translated by D. C. Lau. New York: Penguin, 1979.

———. *Analects of Confucius*. Translated by Simon Leys. New York: Norton, 1997.

Csordas, Thomas J. "The Body as Representation and Being in the World." In *Embodiment and Experience: the Existential Ground of Culture and Self,* edited by Csordas, 1–24. Cambridge: Cambridge University Press, 1994.

Cyphert, Dale. "Ideology, Knowledge and Text: Pulling at the Knot in Ariadner's Thread." *Quarterly Journal of Speech* 84, no. 4 (2001): 378–95.

Dai Changzheng. "Lun zhongguo chuantong zhengzhi wenhua de zhuyao tezheng" [On the Main Features of Chinese Political Culture]. *Xin shiye* [Expanding Horizons], no. 2 (2002): 69–71.

"Daxuesheng shiye: zhongguo shehui de ranmei zhiji" [The Unemployment of Chinese College Graduates: The Anxiety of Chinese Society]. Online at http://www.my.cnd.org/modules/mysection/print.php?articleid=14770 (accessed October 2, 2006)

De Bary, Wm. Theodore. "Individualism and Humanitarianism in the Ming Thought." In *Self and Society in Ming Thought*, edited by de Bary, 145–245. New York: Columbia University Press, 1970.

———. "Some Common Tendencies in Neo-Confucianism." In *Confucianism in Action*, edited by David S. Nivison and Arthur F. Wright, 25–49. Stanford: Stanford University Press, 1959.

De Bary, Wm. Theodore, and Richard Lufrano. *Sources of Chinese Tradition from 1600 through the Twentieth Century*. 2nd ed. New York: Columbia University Press, 2000.

Deng Xiaoping. "Jiefang sixiang, shishiqiushi, tuanjie yizhi, xiangqiankan" [Liberalize Our Thinking, Be Truthful, Unite, and Look Forward]. In *Deng Xiaoping wenxuan* [Selected Writings of Deng Xiaoping]. 3 vols. Beijing: Zhonggong zhongyang wenxian chubanshe, 1994. 3:140–53.

———. "Shehui zhuyi he shichang jingji bu cunzai genben maodun" [There Is No Fundamental Conflict between Socialism and Market Economy]. In *Deng Xiaoping wenxuan* [Selected Writings of Deng Xiaoping]. 3 vols. Beijing: Zhonggong zhongyang wenxian chubanshe, 1994. 3:148–51.

Department of Chinese Language, Wuhan University, ed. *Sanbanshou xinxuan tangshi* [Three Hundred Newly Selected Tong Poems]. Beijing: Renmin chubanshe, 1986.

Deutsch, Eliot. "The Concept of Body." In *Self as Body in Asian Theory and Practice*, edited by Thomas Kasulis with Roger T. Ames and William Dissanayake, 5–19. Albany: State University of New York Press, 1993.

Dewey, John. *Experience and Nature*. New York: Dover, 1958.

"Diaocha 'laisheng shifou yuanzuo zhongguoren, wangzhan zhubian tuzao jiegu" [Survey on if One Wants to Be Chinese in the Next Life Causes Trouble. Editor of Blog Is Fired]. Online at http://my.cnd//modules/mfsection/print/php?articleid=1492 (accessed October 1, 2006)

Dickson, Bruce J. *Red Capitalists in China: The Party, Private Entrepreneurs, and Prospects for Political Change*. Cambridge: Cambridge University Press, 2003.

Dillistone, F. W. "The Relationship between Form and Content: Medium and Message in Christian Communication." In *Art and Religion as Communication*, edited by James Waddell and F. W. Dillistone, 117–36. Atlanta: John Knox Press, 1974.

Ding, X. L. *The Decline of Communism in China: Legitimacy Crisis*. New York: Cambridge University Press, 1994.

Dixon, John W., Jr. "The Way into Matter." In *Art and Religion as Communication*, edited by James Waddell and F. W. Dillistone, 19–50. Atlanta: John Knox Press, 1974.

Dworkin, Ronald. "Taking Rights Seriously in Beijing." *New York Review of Books*, September 26, 2002.

"Eleven Falun Gong Members Arrested for Posting Torture Photos on Internet." *Reports without Borders*. Online at http://www.rsf.org/article.php3?id_article=12170 (accessed July 16, 2010).

Erikson, Erik H. *Identity: Youth and Crisis*. New York: Norton, 1968.

Evans, Sara. *Personal Politics*. New York: Knopf, 1979.

Ewing, Richard Daniel. "Hu Jintao: The Making of a Chinese General Secretary." *China Quarterly* 173 (2003): 17–34.

Fagen, Richard R. *The Transformation of Political Culture in Cuba*. Stanford: Stanford University Press, 1969.

"Falii bixu zhansheng xiejiao" [Law Must Defeat Cult]. *People's Daily*, overseas edition, December 27, 1999.

"Falun gong jiushi xiejiao" [Falun Gong Is a Cult]. *People's Daily*, overseas edition, October 28, 1999.

Fang Litian. "Zhongguo fojiaoxue de xiandai jiazhi" [The Modern Value of the Chinese Buddhist Philosophy]. *Zhongguo renmin daxue xuebao*, no. 4 (2002): 31–39.

Fewsmith, Joseph. *China since Tiananmen: The Politics of Transition*. Cambridge: Cambridge University Press, 2001.

Firth, Raymond. *Religion: A Humanist Interpretation*. London & New York: Routledge, 1996.

Fisher, Walter. "Narration as a Human Communication Paradigm: The Case of Public Moral Argument." In *Contemporary Rhetorical Theory: A Reader*, edited by John Louis Lucaites, Celeste Michelle Condit, and Sally Caudit, 265–87. New York: Guildford Press, 1999.

Franke, William. "Metaphor and the Making of Sense: The Contemporary Metaphor Renaissance." *Philosophy and Rhetoric* 33, no.2 (2000): 137–53.

"French Police Arrest American, UK, Danish, French Citizens for 'Wearing Yellow' during State Visit." *Falun Dafa Information Center*. January 29, 2004. Online at http://faluninfo.net/displayAnArticle.asp?ID=8287 (accessed July 15, 2010).

Friedman, Thomas L. *The Lexus and the Olive Tree*. New York: Farrar, Straus, Giroux, 1999.

Fu Ningjiu. *Kexue zhi jian: He Zuoxiu yuanshi zhuangji* [The Sword of Science: A Biography of He Zuoxiu]. Nanjing: Jiangsu renmin chubanshe, 2000.

"Full Text of Premier Wen's Speech at Harvard: 'Turning Your Eyes to China.'" Online at www.news.harvard.edu/gazette/2003/12.11/10-wenspeak.html (accessed May 31, 2005).

Fung Yu-Lan (Feng Youlan). *A History of Chinese Philosophy*. Translated by Derk Bodde. 2 vols. Princeton: Princeton University Press, 1953.

Gao, Ge, and Xiaosui Xiao. "Intercultural/Interpersonal Research in China: A Preliminary Review." In *Chinese Communication Theory and Research: Reflections, New Trends, and New Directions*, edited by Wenshan Jian, Xing Lu, and D. Ray Heisey, 21–35. Westport, Colo: Ablex, 2002.

Gao Gao and Yan Jiaqi. *Wenge shinianshi* [The Ten-Year History of the Cultural Revolution]. Tianjin: Tianjin chubanshe, 1986.

Gao Xin. *Wen Jiabao zhuan* [Biography of Wen Jiabao]. Carle Place, N.Y.: Mirror Books, 2004.

Gaonkar, Dilip. "The Idea of Rhetoric in the Rhetoric of Science." In *Rhetorical Hermeneutics: Invention and Interpretation in the Age of Science*, edited by Alan G. Gross and William M. Keith, 25–88. Albany: State University of New York Press, 1997.

———. "The Very Idea of a Rhetorical Culture." *Quarterly Journal of Speech* 80 (August 1994): 333–38.

Geertz, Clifford. *The Interpretation of Cultures*. New York: Basic Books, 1973.

Gernet, Jacques. *Buddhism in Chinese Society: An Economic History from the Fifth to the Tenth Centuries*. Translated by Franciscus Verellen. New York: Columbia University Press, 1995.

Giddens, Anthony. *Modernity and Self-Identity*. Stanford: Stanford University Press, 1991.

Giles, John, Albert Park, and Fang Cai. "How Has Economic Restructuring Affected China's Urban Workers." *China Quarterly* 185 (2006): 61–95.

Goldman, Merle, and Roderick MacFarquhar, eds. *The Paradox of China's Post-Mao Reforms*. Cambridge, Mass.: Harvard University Press, 1999.

Gould, Thomas. *The Ancient Quarrel between Poetry and Philosophy*. Princeton: Princeton University Press, 1990.

Grieder, Jerome B. *Intellectuals and the State in Modern China*. New York: Free Press, 1981.

Gross, Alan G. *The Rhetoric of Science*. Cambridge, Mass.: Harvard University Press, 1996.

Gudykunst, William B., and Stella Ting-Toomey. *Culture and Interpersonal Communication*. Newbury Park, Calif.: Sage, 1988.

Gyatso, Janet. "The Ins and Outs of Self-Transformation: Personal and Social Sides of Visionary Practice in Tibetan Buddhism." In *Self and Self-Transformation in the History of Religions*, edited by David Shulman and Guy G. Stroumsa, 183–94. Oxford & New York: Oxford University Press, 2002.

Hahn, Robert. *Sickness and Healing: An Anthropological Perspective*. New Haven: Yale University Press, 1995.

Hakfoort, Casper. "The Historiography of Scientism: A Critical Review." *History of Science* 33 (December 1995): 375–95.

Handelman, Don. "Postlude: The Interior Sociality of Self-Transformation." In *Self and Self-Transformation in the History of Religions*, edited by David Shulman and Guy G. Stroumsa, 236–54. Oxford & New York: Oxford University Press, 2002.

Haraway, Donna. *Simians, Cyborgs, and Women: The Reinvention of Nature*. New York: Routledge, 1990.

Harris, Randy Allen, ed. *Landmark Essays on Rhetoric of Science: Case Studies*. Mahwah, N.J.: Lawrence Erlbaum, 1997.

Hart, Roderick. "The Rhetoric of the True Believer." *Speech Monographs* 38, no.4 (1971): 249–61.

He, Baogang, "Village Citizenship in China: A Case Study of Zhejiang," *Citizenship Studies* 9 (May 2005): 205–19.

He Xin. *Lun zhongguo lishi yu guomin yishi* [On Chinese History and National Conscience]. Beijing: Shishi chubanshe, 2002.

————. *Sikao: Wode zhexue yu zongjiaoguan* [Reflection: My Philosophical and Religious Views]. Beijing: Shishi chubanshe, 2001.

————. *Zhongnanhai miza* [Secret Letters to Zhongnanhai]. Hong Kong: Mingjing chubanshe, 1997.

He Zuoxiu. *Wo bu xinxie: He Zuoxiu fan weikexue lunwenji* [I Do Not Believe in Evil: A Collection of Works by He Zuoxiu on Pseudoscience]. Nanchang: Jiangxi jiaoju chubanshe, 1999.

Heiden, Konrad. *Der Fuehrer: Hitler's Rise to Power.* Translated by Ralph Manheim. Boston: Houghton Mifflin, 1944.

Hertz, Karl. "The Nature of Voluntary Association." In *Voluntary Associations: A Study of Groups in Free Societies,* edited by D. B. Robertson, 17–35. Richmond, Va.: John Knox Press, 1966.

Hill, Thomas E. *Autonomy and Self-Respect.* Cambridge: Cambridge University Press, 1991.

Hoffman, Manfred. "Erasmus: Rhetorical Theologian." In *Rhetorical Invention and Religious Inquiry: New Perspectives,* edited by Walter Jost and Wendy Olmsted, 136–61. New Haven: Yale University Press, 2000.

Holton, Gerald. *The Advancement of Science and Its Burdens.* Cambridge, Mass.: Harvard University Press, 1998.

————. *The Scientific Imagination.* Cambridge, Mass.: Harvard University Press, 1998.

Hook, Brian ed. *The Individual and the State in China.* Oxford & New York: Clarendon Press, 1996.

Hsu, Francis L. K. "The Self in Cross-Cultural Perspective." In *Culture and Self: Asian and Western Perspectives,* edited by Anthony J. Marsella, George DeVos, and Francis L. K. Hsu, 24–55. New York: Tavistock, 1985.

Hu Chengpeng. "Ruoshi qunti—zhongguo muqian jixu jiejue de wenti" [A Socially Vulnerable Group: An Urgent Issue That Needs to Be Solved Right Away in China]. *Journal of Harbin Party School of the CCP,* no. 4 (2002): 51–52.

"Hu Delivers New Year's Message." *China Daily.* Online at http://www.chinadaily.com.cn/English/doc/2005-01/01/content_405151.html (accessed Janury 12, 2005).

Hu Fayun. "Hong luyi" [Red Art Institute of Lu Xun]. In *1966: women nayidai de huiyi* [1966: Recollections of Our Generation], edited by Xu Youyu, 205–30- Beijing: Zhongguo wenlian chubanshe, 1998.

Hu Ping. *Chanji: 1957 kunan de jitan* [Changji: The Altar of Tribulation in 1957]. Guangzhou: Guangdong liiyou chubanshe, 2004.

————. "Cong falun gong xiangxiang tanqi (shang)" [On the Falun Gong Phenomenon, part 1]. *Beijing Spring,* no. 4 (2000): 31–36.

Hu Sheng, ed. *The Seventy-Year History of the Chinese Communist Party.* Beijing: History of CCP Publishing House, 1991.

Hua, Shiping. *Scientism and Humanism: Two Cultures in Post-Mao China, 1978–1989.* Albany: State University of New York Press, 1995.

Hua, Shiping, and Joseph Fewsmith, eds. *Chinese Political Culture: 1989–2000.* Armonk, N.Y.: Sharpe, 2001.

Huang Xiaoshi. "Fojiao rujiao lunli daode jianlun" [A Brief Discussion on the Ethics of Buddhism and Confucianism]. *Sichuan daxue xuebao,* no. 2 (1998): 100–103.

"Huangdan de xieshuo, xian e de yongxin" [Ludicrous Heresy and Evil Intent]. *People's Daily,* overseas edition, August 18, 1999.

"Huifu gaokao sanshinian: luqu xuesheng 3,600 wan" [Thirty Years after the Restoration of Tertiary Education System, 36 Million Students are Admitted]. *People's Daily*, overseas edition, May 5, 2007.

Huntington, Samuel. *The Third Wave, Democratization of the Late Twentieth Century.* Norman: University of Oklahoma Press, 1991.

"International Falun Gong Plaintiffs Win Torture Lawsuits: US Judge Rules Sovereign Immunity Does Not Apply to Perpetrators of Falun Gong Persecution." Online at www.faluninfo.net (accessed December 19, 2004).

Irons, Edward. "Falun Gong and the Sectarian Religion Paradigm." *Nova Religio* 6 (April 2003): 244–62.

James, William. *Writings, 1902–1910.* New York: Library of America, 1987.

Jamieson, Kathleen Hall. "The Metaphoric Cluster in the Rhetoric of Pope Paul VI and Edmund G. Brown, Jr." *Quarterly Journal of Speech* 66 (February 1980): 51–72.

"Jianchi congyan zhidang" [Insist on a Strict Administration of Our Party]. *People's Daily*, overseas edition, July 26, 1999.

Jiang Pei, ed. *Laoxinwen* [Old News]. Tianjing: Tianjing renmin chubanshe, 1998.

Jiang Zemin. "Speech to Commemorate the Eightieth Anniversary of the Founding of the Chinese Communist Party." *People's Daily*, overseas edition, July 1, 2001.

Jiao Wufeng, and Li Xiaoguang. "Dui ruoshiqunti yuyi teshubaohu de faliixue sikao" [Reflection on the Special Legal Protection for the Socially Vulnerable Group]. *Leshan shifan xueyuan xuebao*, no. 9 (2003): 111–15.

"Jiepi Li Hongzhi jiqi 'Falun dafa' shi yichang yansu de zhengzhi douzheng" [To Denounce Li Hongzhi and His 'Falun dafa' Is a Serious Political Struggle]. *People's Daily*, August 2, 1999.

Johnson, Ian. "A Deadly Exercise: Practicing Falun Gong Was a Right, Ms Chen Said, to Her Last Day." *Wall Street Journal*, April 20, 2000, A1.

———. *Wild Grass: Three Stories of Change in Modern China.* New York: Pantheon, 2004.

Jones, Charles B. "Transitions in the Practice and Defense of Chinese Pure Land Buddhism." In *Buddhism in the Modern World: Adaptations of an Ancient Tradition*, edited by Steven Heine and Charles S. Prebish, 123–42. New York: Oxford University Press, 2003.

Jones, James W. *Contemporary Psychoanalysis and Religion: Transference and Transcendence.* New Haven: Yale University Press, 1991.

Kai kou bian xiao. "Cong sanjunzi de zuofu dan wemen zenyang kan zhengfu" [On How to View Our Government after the Arrest of the Three Gentlemen]. Online at *cnd.org.* http://my.cnd.org/modules/wfsection/print.php?articleid=8888 (accessed January 7, 2005).

Keith, Ronald, and Zhiqiu Lin. "The 'Falun Gong Problem': Politics and the Struggle for the Rule of Law in China." *China Quarterly* 175 (2003): 623–42.

Kleinman, Arthur. *Patients and Healers in the Context of Culture: An Exploration of the Borderland between Anthropology, Medicine, and Psychiatry.* Berkeley: University of California Press, 1981.

Kleinman, Arthur, and Joan Kleinman, "Somatization: The Interconnections in Chinese Society among Culture, Depressive Meanings, and the Experience of Pain." In *Culture and Depression*, edited by Arthur Kleinman and Byron Good, 429–90. Berkeley: University of California Press, 1985.

Kleinman, Arthur, Veena Das, and Magaret Lock, eds. *Social Suffering.* Berkeley: University of California Press, 1997.

Kuan Tzu: 24 Chuan/Fang Hsuan-ling. Ssu pu pei yao edition, 16.4a–b. Shanghai: Shangwu yinshuguan, 1922.

Kubin, Wolfgang. "On the Problem of the Self in Confucianism." In *Confucianism and the Modernization of China,* edited by Silke Krieger and Rolf Trauzettel, 63–95. Mainz: Hase & Koehler, 1991.

Kurlantzick, Joshua. *Charm Offensive: How China's Soft Power Is Transforming the World.* New Haven: Yale University Press, 2007.

Kwok, D. W. Y. *Scientism in Chinese Thought, 1900–1950.* New Haven: Yale University Press, 1965.

Lacan, Jacques. *Ecritis: A Selection.* Translated by Alan Sheridan. New York: Norton, 1978.

Lakoff, George, and Mark Johnson. *Metaphors We Live By.* Chicago: Chicago University Press, 1980.

Lam, Willy Wo-Lap. *The Era of Jiang Zemin.* Singapore: Prentice Hall, 1999.

Lambert, Malcolm. *Medieval Heresy.* 2nd ed. Oxford: Blackwell, 1992.

Lehning, James R. *To Be a Citizen: The Political Culture of the Early French Third Republic.* Ithaca, N.Y.: Cornell University Press, 2001.

Lei Feng. *Lei Feng riji* [The Diary of Lei Feng]. Hong Kong: Chaoyang chubanshe, 1969.

"A Letter Home." *Falun dafa* (Falun Gong publication), no. 6 (2000).

Li Changping. *Wo xiang zongli shuo shihua* [I Told the Premier the Truth]. Beijing: Guangming ribao chubanshe, 2002.

Li Hongzhi. *Falun fofa.* Hong Kong: Falun Fofa Publishing House, 1998.

———. *Hong Yin* [Grand Poetry]. Taipei: Yiqun Books, 2003.

———. *Zhuan Falun* [The Turning Wheel of the Law]. Beijing: Zhongguo guangbo dianshi chubanshe, 1994.

"Li Hongzhi fabiao 'wo de yidian shengming': xianzai he jianglai dou buhui fandui zhengfu" [Li Hongzhi Issued "My Statement: I Will Never Oppose the Government Now or in the Future"]. *World Journal,* July 23, 1999.

Li Rui. *Zhiyan: Li Rui liushinian de you yu si* [Honest Speech: Li Rui's Concern and Reflection on Sixty Years]. Beijing: Jinri zhongguo chubanshe, 1998.

Li Weixing. "Bugei cuowu sixiang tigong chuanbo qudao, zhendi yishi zhiguan zhongyao" [We Must Not Provide Channels for Erroneous Thoughts. It Is Important to Safeguard the Ideological Front]. Online at http://www.people.com.cn/GB/shizheng/1026/3027154.html (accessed June 12, 2005).

Li Yixiang. "Yige boshisheng yu fanlungong de juelie" [How a Ph.D. Student Broke His Ties with Falun Gong]. *People's Daily,* overseas edition, January 5, 2000.

Li Youning. *Wuhan Zhuan* [A Biography of Wu Han]. Hong Kong: Mingbao yuekan chubanshe, 1973.

Liang Shuming. *Ruxue fuxing zhilu: Liang Shuming wenxuan* [The Confucian Road to Restoration: Selected Writings of Liang Shuming]. Edited by Cao Jingqing. Shanghai: Shanghai yuandong chubanshe, 1994.

Liao Yiwu. *Shehui diceng fangtanlu* [Voice from the Lowest Rung of the Society]. 3 vols. Taipei: Maitian chubanshe, 2002.

Liebman, Benjamin. "Watchdogs or Demagogues? The Media in the Chinese Legal System," *Columbia Law Review* 105 (January 2005): 1–157.

"Lilun yantai: zenyang bawo yulun daoxiang, zengqang yingdao yulun de benlin" [How Do We Direct Public Opinion and Develop Our Ability to Channel Public Opinion]. Online at http://www.people.com.cn/GB/shizheng/1026/3054959.html (accessed June 12, 2005).

Lin, Chun. *The Transformation of Chinese Socialism*. Durham: Duke University Press, 2006.

Lin, Min, and Maria Galikowski. *The Search for Modernity: Chinese Intellectuals and Cultural Discourse in the Post-Mao Era*. New York: St. Martin's Press, 1999.

Lin, Yutang. *My Country and My People*. New York: Reynal & Hitchcock, 1935.

Lin Feng. *Zhonggong fengyu bashinian* [Eighty Years of Wind and Rain for the Chinese Communist Party]. Edison, N. J.: Epoch, 2001.

Lin Zhijun. *Bianhua: Liusi zhijin de zhongguo shehui damaidong* [Change: The Pulse of Chinese Society since June Fourth]. Taipei: Shibao wenhua chubanshe, 2003.

Liu, Yameng. "Three Issues in the Argumentative Conception of Early Chinese Discourse." *Philosophy East and West* 46, no. 1 (1996): 33–58.

Liu, Yingqin. "Cultural Factors and Rhetorical Patterns in Classical Chinese Argumentation." *Intercultural Communication Studies* 16, no.1 (2007): 197–204.

Liu Binyan. *A Higher Kind of Loyalty: A Memoir by Chinese Foremost Journalist*. New York: Pantheon, 1990.

Liu Guanjun. "Lun Jiang Zemin bianzheng weiwu zhuyi kexueguan de neihan" [On Jiang Zemin's Outlook of Dialectic Materialism and Science and Technology]. *Journal of Shandong Teachers' University* (Humanities and Social Science edition) 47, no. 1 (2002): 9–13.

Liu Peiqi. "Renwen zhuyi yu lixing zhuyi zhi bijiao" [A Comparison between Humanism and Rationalism]. *Reference Teaching to Middle School History* 11 (2002): 33.

Liu Sanfu. "Rujiao daode tixi yu shidai wenhua jingshen de jiazhi cuowei" [The Mismatch between the Confucian Ethical System and Contemporary Cultural Spirit]. *Jilin daxue shehui kexue xuebao*, no. 3 (1995): 58–62.

Liu Shaoqi. "How to Be a Good Communist." In *Selected Works of Liu Shaoqi*, 107–67. Beijing: Foreign Language Press, 1984.

Liu Xiaobo. "Renquan yishi de juexing yu zhengzhi gaige" [On the Awakening of Human Rights Conscience and Political Reform]. Beijing Spring, no. 2 (2003): 41–47.

Liu Xiaoting. "Dui kexue yu zongjiao huanxi guanxi de zhishi shehui fenxi" [On the Relationship between Science and Religion]. *Hebei Academic Journal*. 27, no.3 (2007): 43–48.

Lu, Xing. "Chinese Political Communication: Roots in Asian and Impacts on Contemporary Chinese Thought and Culture." *Intercultural Communication Studies* 11, no. 1 (2002): 97–116.

———. *Rhetoric in Ancient China: Fifth to Third Century B.C.E.* Columbia: South Carolina Press, 1998.

———. *Rhetoric of the Chinese Cultural Revolution: The Impact on Chinese Thought, Culture, and Communication*. Columbia: University of South Carolina Press, 2004.

Lu, Xing, and Herbert Simons. "Traditional Rhetoric of Chinese Communist Party Leaders in the Post Mao Reform Period: Dilemmas and Strategies." *Quarterly Journal of Speech* 92 (August 2006): 262–86.

Luo Bin. "Yinmo zhenya falun gong de neimu" [The Inside Story of the Plot to Suppress Falun Gong]. *Zhengming* 262 (1999): 6–8.

Lyon, M. L., and J. M. Barbalet. "Society's Body: Emotion and 'Somatization' of Social Theory." In *Embodiment and Experience: The Existential Ground of Culture and Self,* edited by Thomas Csordas, 148–66. Cambridge: Cambridge University Press, 2003.

Ma Ling, and Li Ming. *Wen Jiabao.* Taipei: Lianjing chubanshe, 2003.

MacInnis, Donald E. *Religion in China Today: Policy and Practice.* New York: Orbis, 1989.

Madsen, Richard. "The Spiritual Crisis of China's Intellectuals." In *Chinese Society on the Eve of Tiananmen,* edited by Deborah Davis and Ezra Vogel, 243–60. Cambridge, Mass.: Harvard University Press, 1990.

Mannheim, Karl. *Ideology and Utopia.* London: Kegan Paul / New York, Harcourt, Brace, 1936.

Mao, LuMing. "Reflective Encounters: Illustrating Comparative Rhetoric." *Style* 37 (Winter 2003): 1–18.

Mao Zedong. "Opposing Stereotyped Party Writing." In *Selected Works of Mao Tse-tung,* 4 vols. Beijing: Foreign Language Press, 1965. 3:53–68.

———. "Rectify the Party's Style of Work." In *Selected Works of Mao Tse-tung,* 3:35–51.

———. "The Report at the Second Plenary Meeting of the Seventh Central Committee of the Chinese Communist Party." In *Selected Works of Mao Tse-tung,* 4:361–75.

———. "Shijianlun" [On Practice]. In *Selected Works of Mao Tse-tung,* 1:295–309.

———. "Talks at the Yenan Forum of Literature and Art." *Selected Works of Mao Tse-tung,* 3:69–98.

Margalit, Avishai. *The Decent Society.* Translated by Naomi Goldblum. Cambridge, Mass.: Harvard University Press, 1996.

Markus, Hazel, Marie Crane, Stan Bernstein, and Michael Siladi. "Self-Schemas and Gender." *Journal of Personality and Social Psychology* 42 (January 1982): 38–50.

McGee, Michael Calvin. "In Search of 'the People': A Rhetorical Alternative." In *Contemporary Rhetorical Theory: A Reader,* edited by John Louis Lucaites, Celeste Michelle Condit, and Sally Caudit, 341–56. New York: Guildford Press, 1999.

McKerrow, Raymie. "Critical Rhetoric: Theory and Praxis." In *Contemporary Rhetorical Theory: A Reader,* edited by John Louis Lucaites, Celeste Michelle Condit, and Sally Caudit, 441–63. New York: Guildford Press, 1999.

Mencius. Harvard-Yenching Index series 57.7B.25.

Merton, Robert K. *The Sociology of Science: Theoretical and Empirical Investigations.* Chicago: University of Chicago Press, 1973.

Metzger, Thomas A. *Escape from Predicament: Neo-Confucianism and China's Evolving Political Culture.* New York: Columbia University Press, 1977.

Miike, Yoshitaka. "An Anatomy of Eurocentrism in Communication Scholarship: The Role of Asiacentricity in De-Westernizing Theory and Research." *China Media Research* 6, no. 1 (2010): 1–11.

Miller, Brett A. "Seeing through a Glass Darkly: Religious Metaphor as Rhetorical Perspective." *Journal of Communication and Religion* 22, no. 2 (1999): 214–36.

Mills, Doug. "Bush and Hu Vow New Cooperation." *New York Times*, April 21, 2006.

"Mitu zhifan" [Coming Back from a Wrong Road]. *People's Daily*, overseas edition, July 31,1999.

Morris, David. "About Suffering: Voice, Genre, and Moral Community." In *Social Suffering*, edited by Arthur Kleinman, Veena Das, and Margaret Lock, 25–45. Berkeley: University of California Press, 1997.

"Muqinjie jiyu" [On Mother's Day], *Qingliu* (Falun Gong publication), no. 23 (May 2003): 7.

Naquin, Susan, and Evelyn S. Rawski. *Chinese Society in the Eighteenth Century*. New Haven: Yale University Press, 1987.

Nelson, John. "Political Foundations for the Rhetoric of Inquiry." In *The Rhetorical Turn: Invention and Persuasion in the Conduct of Inquiry*, edited by Herbert Simons, 258–92. Chicago: University of Chicago Press, 1990.

"1988 nian de Shekou Fengbo" [Shekou Storm in 1988]. Online at http://www .douban.com/group/topic/2326691/ (accessed July 27, 2010).

O'Brien, Kevin J. "Neither Transgressive nor Contained: Boundary-Spanning Contention in China." *Mobilization* 8 (February 2003): 51–64.

O'Brien, Kevin J., and Lianjiang Li. *Rightful Resistance in Rural China*. Cambridge: Cambridge University Press, 2006.

Oksenberg, Michel. "China's Political System: Challenges of the Twenty-first Century." *The Nature of Chinese Politics*. Edited by Jonathan Unger, 193–208. Armonk, N.Y.: Sharpe, 2002.

Overmyer, Daniel. *Folk Buddhist Religion: Dissenting Sects in Late Traditional China*. Cambridge, Mass.: Harvard University Press, 1976.

Ownby, David. "The Audience: Growing Alienation among Chinese Youths." In *China's Establishment Intellectuals*, edited by Carol Lee Hamrin and Timothy Creek, 212–46. Armonk, N.Y.: Sharpe, 1986.

———. *Falun Gong and the Future of China*. New York: Oxford University Press, 2008.

———. "A History for Falun Gong: Popular Religion and the Chinese State since the Ming Dynasty." *Nova Religio* 6 (April 2003): 223–43.

Ozouf, Mona. "'Public Opinion' at the End of the Old Regime." *Journal of Modern History* 60, supplement (September 1988): S1–S21.

Padel, Ruth. *In and Out of the Mind: Greek Images of the Tragic Self*. Princeton: Princeton University Press, 1992.

Pan Xiao. "Why Is the Road to Life Narrower and Narrower?" (letter to the editor). *China Youth*, no. 5 (1980): 3–5.

Pei, Minxin. *From Reform to Revolution: The Demise of Communism in China and the Soviet Union*. Cambridge, Mass.: Harvard University Press, 1994.

———. *China's Trapped Transition: The Limits of Developmental Autocracy*. Cambridge, Mass.: Harvard University Press, 2006.

Perry, Elizabeth, and Mark Selden, eds. *Chinese Society: Change, Conflict, and Resistance*. New York: Routledge, 2000.

Polletta, Francesca. "'Free Spaces' in Collective Action." *Theory and Society* 28 (1999): 1–38.

Porter, Noah. *Falun Gong in the United States: An Ethnographic Study*. Parkland, Fla.: Dissertation.com, 2003.

Potter, Pitman. "Belief in Control: Regulation of Religion in China." *China Quarterly* 174 (2003): 317–37.

Powers, John, and Meg Y. M. Lee. "Dueling Media: Symbolic Conflict in China's Falun Gong Suppression Campaign." In *Chinese Conflict Management and Resolution*, edited by Guo-ming Chen and Ringo Ma, 259–74. Westport, Conn.: Ablex, 2002.

Psychological Research Institute of the Chinese Academy of Science. *Falun gong xianxiang de xinlixue fenxi* [A Psychological Analysis of the Falun Gong Phenomenon]. Beijing: Kexue chuban she, 2002.

Pye, Lucian W. *The Spirit of Chinese Politics*. Cambridge, Mass.: Harvard University Press, 1992.

————. "The State and the Individual: An Overview Interpretation." In *The Individual and State in China*, edited by Brian Hook, 16–42. Oxford: Clarendon Press, 1996.

Pye, Lucian, and Sidney Verba, eds. *Political Culture and Political Development*. Princeton: Princeton University Press, 1965.

"Qinmin aimin zhengfu xingxiang: Wen Jiaobao sange xinnian zhuyuan" [Creating an Official Image of Being Close to People and Loving People: Three New Year Promises of Wen Jiabao]. *Zhenzhou Wanbao*. Online at http://cn.news.yahoo.com/050218/346/292da_4html (accessed 2006).

Qisu Jiang Zemin [Suing Jiang Zemin]. Taipei: Jinglianhua chubanshe, 2003.

Qu Weiguo. "Weiji or Jinbu?" [Crisis or Progress?]. In *Renwen jingshen xunsilu* [Writings on Pursuing and Reflecting on Humanistic Spirit], 100–105. Shanghai: Wenhui chubanshe, 1996.

"Quanguo gedi ganbu qunchong biaoshi jianjue yonghu dang he zhengfu chuli falun gong wenti de jueding" [Cadres and Masses from All over the Country Support How the Party and the Government Deal with Falun Gong], *People's Daily*, July 24, 1999.

Regan, Tom. *Three Generation: Reflections on the Coming Revolution*. Philadelphia: Temple University Press, 1991.

Ren Buxou. "Hu Jintao shidai de xinling saodong" [The Emotional Commotion during the Time of Hu Jintao]. Online at http://my.cnd.org/modules/wfsection/print.php?articleid=8872 (accessed January 11, 2005).

Roof, Wade Clark. *Spiritual Marketplace: Baby Boomers and the Remaking of American Religion*. Princeton: Princeton University Press, 1999.

Rosen, Stanley. "Youth and Social Change in the PRC." In *Two Societies in Opposition: The Republic of China and the People's Republic of China after Forty Years*, edited by Ramon H. Myers, 288–315. Stanford: Hoover Institution Press, Stanford University, 1991.

Rosenthal, Elizabeth. "Falun Gong Holds Protests on Anniversary of Big Sit-In," *New York Times*, April 26, 2001.

Rosteck, Thomas. "Approaching the Intersection: Issues of Identity, Politics, and Critical Practice." In *At the Intersection: Cultural Studies and Rhetorical Studies*, edited by Thomas Rosteck, 1–23. New York: Guilford Press, 1999.

————. "A Cultural Tradition in Rhetorical Studies." In *At the Intersection: Cultural Studies and Rhetorical Studies*, edited by Thomas Rosteck, 226–47. New York: Guilford Press, 1999.

Rothbard, Murray N. "The Mantle of Science." In *Scientism and Values*, edited by Helmut Schoeck and James W. Wiggins, 159–80. Princeton: Van Nostrand, 1960.

Ru, Xin, ed. *1999: Zhongguo shehui xingshi fenxi yu yuce* [1999: An Analysis and Predictions of Chinese Social Situation]. Beijing: Shehui kexue wenxian chubanshe, 1999.

Rudolph, Susanne H. *Transnational Religion and Fading States*. Boulder, Colo.: Westview Press, 1997.

Sange daibiao [Three Represents]. Taipei: Qisi chubanshe, 2003.

Schechter, Danny. *Falun Gong's Challenge to China*. New York: Akashic Books, 2000.

Scheper-Hughes, Nancy, and Margaret Lock. "The Mindful Body: A Prolegomenon to Future Work in Medical Anthropology." *Medical Anthropology Quarterly*, n.s., 1 (March 1987): 6–41.

Schoeck, Helmut. Introduction to *Scientism and Values*, edited by Helmut Schoeck and James W. Wiggins. Princeton: Van Nostrand, 1960.

Schoenhals, Michael. *Doing Things with Words in Chinese Politics: Five Case Studies*. Berkeley: University of California Press, 1992.

Schwartz, Benjamin. "Some Polarities in Confucian Thought." In *Confucianism in Action*, edited by David S. Nivison and Arthur F. Wright, 50–62. Stanford: Stanford University Press, 1959.

Scott, James C. *Domination and the Arts of Resistance*. New Haven: Yale University Press, 1990.

———. *Weapons of the Weak: Everyday Forms of Peasant Resistance*. New Haven: Yale University Press, 1985.

Shang, Xiaoyuan, Xiaoming Wu, and Yue Wu. "Welfare Provisions for Vulnerable Children: The Missing Role of the State." *China Quarterly* 181 (2005): 122–36.

Shang Jiuyun. "Shilun zhongjiao zhi gongneng" [On the Function of Religion]. *Journal of Zhengzhou University*, no. 4 (1997): 53–57.

"Shehui de duliu, renmin de huohai" [Cancer of Society and Curse of the People]. *People's Daily*, overseas edition, August 20, 1999.

Shek, Richard. "The Alternative Moral Universe of Religious Dissenters in Ming-Qing China." In *Religion and the Early Modern State: Views from China, Russia, and the West*, edited by James D. Tracy and Marguerite Ragnow, 13–51. Cambridge & New York: Cambridge University Press, 2004.

Shek, Richard, and Tetsurō Noguchi. "Eternal Mother Religion: Its History and Ethics." In *Heterodoxy in Late Imperial China*, edited by Shek and Kwang-Ching Liu, 241–80. Honolulu: University of Hawaii Press, 2004.

"Shekou fengbo wendalu" [Shekou Storm Dialogue], *People's Daily*, August 6, 1988.

Sheng Hongyu. "Jianlun shehui zhuyi shichang jingji xia de renge tezheng" [On the Characteristics of Personality under the Socialist Market Economy]. *Journal of Anhui Agricultural University*, no. 1 (2002): 86–88.

Shi, Fayong, and Yongshun Cai. "Disaggregating the State: Networks and Collective Resistance in Shanghai." *China Quarterly* 186 (2006): 314–32.

Shi Mu. "Ni xingfu ma?" [Are You Happy?]. *Epoch Times*, May 5–11, 2003.

Shome, Raka. "Postcolonial Interventions in the Rhetorical Canon." In *Contemporary Rhetorical Theory: A Reader*, edited by John Louis Lucaites, Celeste Michelle Condit, and Sally Caudit, 591–608. New York: Guildford Press, 1999.

Shulman, David, and Guy G. Stroumsa. "Persons, Passages and Shifting Cultural Space." In *Self and Self-Transformation in the History of Religions*, edited by Shulman and Stroumsa, 1–16. Oxford & New York: Oxford University Press, 2002.

———, eds. *Self and Self-Transformation in the History of Religions*. Oxford & New York: Oxford University Press, 2002.

Silverman, Kaja. *The Subject of Semiotics*. New York: Oxford University Press, 1983.

Simmel, Georg. *Essays on Religion*, edited and translated by Horst Jürgen Helle and Ludwig and Nieder. New Haven: Yale University Press, 1997.

Simons, Herbert, ed. *The Rhetorical Turn: Invention and Persuasion in the Conduct of Inquiry*. Chicago: University of Chicago Press, 1990.

Smith, Craig S. "Sect Sues Minister." *New York Times*, January 29, 2004.

Solinger, Dorothy J. "Labor Market Reform and the Plight of the Laid-off Proletariat." *China Quarterly* 170 (2002): 304–26.

Solomon, Richard H. *Mao's Revolution and the Chinese Political Culture*. Ann Arbor: Center for Chinese Studies, University of Michigan, 1998.

Sorell, Tom. *Scientism: Philosophy and the Infatuation with Science*. London & New York: Routledge, 1991.

Spence, Jonathan D. *The Gate of Heavenly Peace: The Chinese People and Their Revolution, 1895–1980*. New York: Penguin, 1981.

Stark, Rodney, and William Sims Bainbridge. *The Future of Religion: Secularization, Revival, and Cult Formation*. Berkeley: University of California Press, 1985.

Stanley, Manfred. "The Rhetoric of the Commons: Forum Discourse in Politics and Society." In *The Rhetorical Turn: Invention and Persuasion in the Conduct of Inquiry*, edited by Herbert Simons, 238–57. Chicago: University of Chicago Press, 1990.

Starosta, William. "Rhetoric and Culture: An Integrative View." *China Media Research* 2, no. 4 (2006): 64–75.

Swidler, Ann. "Culture in Action: Symbols and Strategies." *American Sociological Review* 51, no. 2 (1986): 273–86.

Tang, Wenfang. *Public Opinion and Political Change in China*. Stanford: Stanford University Press, 2005.

Tang Liang. *Jianjin, minzhu: biange zhong de zhongguo zhengzhi* [Progress, Democracy: Chinese Politics amidst Reform]. Singapore: Bafang Cultural Co., 2004.

Tay, William. "'Obscure Poetry': A Controversy in China." In *After Mao: Chinese Literature and Society: 1978–1991*, edited by Jeffrey Kinkley, 133–57. Cambridge, Mass.: Harvard University Press, 1985.

Taylor, Charles Alan. *Defining Science: A Rhetoric of Demarcation*. Madison: University of Wisconsin Press, 1996.

Thireau, Isabelle, and Hua Linshan, "The Moral Universe of Aggrieved Chinese Workers," *China Journal* 50 (July 2003): 83–103.

———. "One Law, Two Interpretations: Mobilizing the Labor Law in Arbitration Committees and in Letters and Visits Office." In *Engaging the Law in China: State, Society and Possibilities for Justice*, edited by Neil Diamant, Stanley Lubman, and Kevin O'Brien, 84–107. Stanford: Stanford University Press, 2005.

Thornton, Patricia M. "Framing Dissent in Contemporary China: Irony, Ambiguity, and Metonymy." *China Quarterly* 171 (2002): 661–81.

Tian Hua. "Lun dangdai shehui fenhua zhong de xinsheng ruoshi qunti" [On the New Socially Vulnerable Group in the Current Social Stratification]. *Academic Exploration*, no. 5 (2001): 52–55.

"Tigao renshi renqing weixie" [Increase Awareness and See the Danger of Falun Gong to the Fullest Extent]. *People's Daily*, overseas edition, July 27, 2001.

Tocqueville, Alexis de. *The Old Régime and the French Revolution*. Translated by Stuart Gilbert. Garden City, N.Y.: Doubleday, 1955.

Tong, James. "An Organizational Analysis of *Falun Gong*: Structure, Communications and Financing," *China Quarterly* 171 (2002): 636–60.

Torrance, Robert M. *The Spiritual Quest*. Berkeley: University of California Press, 1994.

Tsou, Tang. *The Cultural Revolution and Post-Mao Reforms: A Historical Perspective*. Chicago: University of Chicago Press, 1986.

Tu, Weiming. *Centrality and Commonality: An Essay on Confucian Religiousness*. Albany, N.Y.: State University of New York Press, 1989.

Uhalley, Stephen. *A History of the Chinese Communist Party*. Stanford: Hoover Institution Press, 1988.

Waddell, James, and F. W. Dillistone. Introduction to *Art and Religion as Communication*, edited by Waddell and Dilliston. Atlanta: John Knox Press, 1962.

Wander, Philip. "The Third Persona: An Ideological Turn in Rhetorical Theory." In *Contemporary Rhetorical Theory: A Reader*, edited by John Louis Lucaites, Celeste Michelle Condit, and Sally Caudit, 357–79. New York: Guildford Press, 1999.

Wang, Ban. *Illuminations from the Past: Trauma, Memory, and History in Modern China*. Stanford: Stanford University Press, 2004.

Wang, Jing. *High Culture Fever: Politics, Aesthetics, and Ideology in Deng's China*. Berkeley: University of California Press, 1996.

Wang Cailing. "Baohu ruoshi qunti xiandai lunli jiegou de yige zhongyao huanjie" [On Protection of the "Socially Vulnerable Group": A Crucial Step in Building Contemporary Ethical Order]. *Theory Journal* 104, no.4 (2001): 94–95.

Wang Dan. *"Liusi" canjiazhe huiyilu* [Recollections of June 4 Participants]. Carle Place, N.Y.: Mirror Books, 2004.

Wang Meng. "Renwen jingshen wenti yougan" [Reflection on the Issue of Humanism]. *Renwen jingshen xunsilu* [Writings on Pursuing and Reflecting Humanistic Spirit]. Shanghai: Wenhui chubanshe, 1996.

———. *Wo de Rensheng Zhexue* [My Life Philosophy]. Taipei: Lixu wenhua, 2003.

Wang Sibin. "Ruoshi qunti shengcun zhuangkuang de gaishan yu shehui zhengce de tiaozheng" [To Improve the Living Condition of the Socially Vulnerable Group and Adjust Social Policies]. *China Cadres Tribune*, no. 4 (2002): 1–3.

———. "Shehui zhuangxing zhong de ruoshi qunti" [On Socially Vulnerable Groups]. *China Cadres Tribune*, no.3 (2002): 4–7.

Wang Youqun. "Guanyu falun gong de yifengxin" [Ten-Thousand-Character Open Letter to Jiang Zemin]. *Beijing Spring* 77 (1999): 24–29.

Wasburn, Philo C. *Broadcasting Propaganda: International Radio Broadcasting and the Construction of Political Reality*. Westport, Conn.: Praeger, 1992.

Watson, Burton, trans. *Chuang Tzu: Basic Writings*. New York: Columbia University Press, 1964.

Weaver, Richard. *The Ethics of Rhetoric*. Chicago: Regnery, 1953.

Wei Chengsi, ed. *Zhongguo dangdai kexue sichao: 1949–1991* [Contemporary Chinese Scientific Trends of Thought: 1949–1991]. Shanghai: Sanlian shudian, 1993.

Wei Liming. "Confucianism: Still a Subject of Interest." *Beijing Review* 32 (December 1989): 21–25.

Weigelin-Schwiedrzik, Susanne. "In Search of a Master Narrative for Twentieth-Century Chinese History." *China Quarterly* 188 (2006): 1070–91.

Weston, Timothy B., and Lionel M. Jensen, eds. *China beyond the Headlines.* Boulder, Colo.: Rowman & Littlefield, 2000.

White, Gordon. "The Dynamics of Civil Society in Post-Mao China." In *The Individual and State in China*, edited by Brian Hook, 196–221. Oxford: Clarendon Press, 1996.

White, Hayden. *The Content of the Form: Narrative Discourse and Historical Representation.* Baltimore: Johns Hopkins University Press, 1990.

———. *Tropics of Discourse: Essays in Cultural Criticism.* Baltimore: John Hopkins University Press, 1985.

Whitehill, James D. "The Indirect Communication: Kierkegaard and Beckett." *Art and Religion as Communication*, edited by James Waddell and F. W. Dillistone, 79–93. Atlanta: John Knox Press, 1962.

Wilkinson, C. A. "The Rhetorical Analysis of Movements: A Process Analysis of the Catonville-Nine Incident." Paper presented at the annual convention of the Central States Speech Association, Detroit, 1977.

Witten, Marsha G. *All Is Forgiven: The Secular Message in American Protestantism.* New York: Princeton University Press, 1993.

Wong, Chack-kie, Vai lo Lo, and Kwong-leung Tang. *China's Urban Health Care Reform: From State Protection to Individual Responsibility.* New York: Lexington Books, 2006.

Wong, John, and William T. Liu. *The Mystery of China's Falun Gong : Its Rise and Sociological Implication.* Singapore City: Singapore University Press, 1999.

Wright, Arthur F. *Studies in Chinese Buddhism.* Edited by Robert M. Somers. New Haven: Yale University Press, 1990.

Wuthnow, Robert. "The Cultural Context of Contemporary Religious Movements." In *Cults, Culture, and Law: Perspectives on New Religious Movement*, edited by Thomas Robbins, William C. Shepherd, and James McBride, 43–56. Chico, Calif.: Scholars Press, 1985.

Xia Guoying. "Lun zhongguo dangdai shehui de lixiang renge" [On the Ideal Personality of Contemporary Chinese Society]. *Jiangxi shehui kexue*, no.3 (2002): 11–13.

Xiao, Xiaosui. "The 1923 Scientific Campaign and Dao Discourse: A Cross-Cultural Study of the Rhetoric of Science." *Quarterly Journal of Speech* 90, no.4 (2004): 469–94.

Xiao Xiaojun. "Buzai weixin" [No Longer Against One's Conscience]. *Falun dafa* (Faun Gong publication), July 2000.

Xing Long. "Gouzao kaifang de renwen jingshen" [Create an Open Humanism]. *Kexue, jishu yu bianzhengfa*, no.12 (2002): 13.

Xu, Ben. *Disenchanted Democracy: Chinese Cultural Criticism after 1989.* Ann Arbor: University of Michigan Press, 1999.

Xu, Jian. "Body, Discourse, and the Cultural Politics of Contemporary Chinese Qigong." *Journal of Asian Studies* 58 (November 1999): 961–91.

Xu, Luo. *Searching for Life's Meaning: Changes and Tensions in the Worldview of Chinese Youth in the 1980s.* Ann Arbor: University of Michigan Press, 2002.

Xu Liangying. *Science and Socialist Construction in China.* Armonk, N.Y.: Sharpe, 1982.

Xu Youyu, ed. *1966: women nayidai de huiyi* [1966: Recollections of Our Generation]. Beijing: Zhongguo wenlian chubanshe, 1998.

Xu Yucheng. "Guanyu woguo shehuizhuyi zongjiao wenti de jiben guandian he jiben zhengce" [Basic Viewpoints and Policies on Religious Issues during Our Country's Socialist Period]. In *Zhongjiao zhengce falü zhishi dawen* [Responses to Questions about Knowledge of Law and Policy on Religion]. Beijing: Chinese Academy of Social Sciences Press, 1997.

Xuan Changnen, "Duoyangxing caineng baozheng wending he huoli" [Only Plurality Can Ensure Stability and Vitality]. *People's Daily*, August 19, 1988, 3.

Yang, C. K. *Religion in Chinese Society: A Study of Contemporary Social Functions of Religion and Some of Their Historical Factors.* Berkeley: University of California Press, 1961.

Yang, Winston L. Y., and Marshal L. Wagner. *Tiananmen: China's Struggle for Democracy.* Baltimore: School of Law, University of Maryland, 1990.

Yang Fan. "'Shekou Fengbo': liangzhong shenceng jiazhiguan de chongtu" ["Shekou Storm": The Contention of Two Profound Values]. *Shekou tongxunbao* [Shekou Post], September 12, 1988.

———. "Shekou fenbo de qianqian houhou" [Events Surrounding the Shekou Storm]. *Zhongguo qingnian* [China Youth], August 5, 1988.

Yang Wei and Chen Hong. "Lun rujia lixiang renge de xue shi jiqi jindai zhuarhuang" [On Defects of Confucian Personality and Their Role in Modern Times]. *Journal of Haerbin Engineering University*, no. 4 (2002): 31–33.

Yao, Qingjiang. "China's Official Framing of Religion and Its Influence on Young Chinese Students: A Partial Testing of the Process of Framing in a Special Media Environment." *Asian Journal of Communication* 17 (December 2007): 416–32.

Yao, Weiqun. "Buddhist Ethical Thought and Modern Society." *Journal of Peking University*, no. 3 (1999): 85–92.

Ye Ning. "Falun gong yi liangzhi huanxing zhonghuaminzu" [Falun Gong Wakes Up Chinese People with Conscience]. *Qingliu* (Falun Gong publication) 27 (January 7, 2004): 3.

Yi Ming. *Hu Wen xin zheng.* Hong Kong: Ming jing chu ban she, 2004.

"Yifa zhiguo, yancheng xiejiao" [Rule the Country by Law and Suppress the Cult Severely]. *People's Daily*, overseas edition, November 1, 1999.

"Yingzao wenming kexue de shehui huanjing" [To Create a Scientific and Civilized Social Environment]. *People's Daily*, overseas edition, August 12, 1999.

"Yiren weiben, guanzhu anquan, guan ai sheng ming" [Treat the People as Central, Pay Attention to Safety, and Be Attentive to Life], *People's Daily*, overseas edition, March 29, 2006.

You, Xiaoye. "The *Way*, Multimodality of Ritual Symbols and Social Change, Reading Confucius's *Analects* as a Rhetoric." *Rhetoric Society Quarterly* 36 (December 2006): 425–48.

Young, John W. *Totalitarian Language: Orwell's Newspeak and Its Nazi and Communist Antecedents.* Charlottesville: University Press of Virginia, 1991.

Yoder, Amos. *Communism in Transition: The End of the Soviet Empires.* Washington, D.C: Taylor & Francis, 1993.

Yu Changmiao and Li Wei. *Shiwuda yihou de zhongguo* [China after the Fifteen Congress of the Chinese Communist Party]. Beijing: Renmi chubanshe,1998.

Yu Fan. "Zhuanxingqi de ruoshi qunti wenti yu women de zhengce xuanze" [On the Issue of the Socially Vulnerable Group and the Selection of Our Policies in the Period of Transition] *Tansuo*, no. 4 (2002): 84–87.

Yu Zhuoli and Zhang Yijui. *Muji: Ershinian zhongguo shijianji* [Firsthand Account: An Annal of Events of the Past Twenty Years in China]. Beijing: Jinji ribao chubanshe, 1998.

Yuan Weishi. "Renwen jingshen zai zhongguo: cong gen jiuqi" [Humanism in China: Save It from the Roots]. In *Renwen jingshen xunsilun* [Writings on Pursuing and Reflecting the Humanistic Spirit], 185–200. Shanghai: Wenhui chubanshe, 1996.

Yurchak, Alexei. *Everything Was Forever, Until It Was No More: The Last Soviet Generation.* Princeton: Princeton University Press, 2006.

"Zai Zhongguo zuo yige qiongren bi si hainanshou" [To Be a Poor Person in China Is Worse than Death]. Online at http://my.cnd.org/modules/wfsection/print.php ?articleid=8869 (accessed January 5, 2005).

Zan Jiansen, "Gaige zhong de 'ruoshi qunti' de chengyin tanxi" [The Search for the Cause of the "Socially Vulnerable Group" in the Economic Reforms]. *Dangdai shijie yu shehui zhuyi* [Contemporary World and Socialism], no.1 (2002): 64–67.

Zhang Dainian. *Zhang Dainian Quanji* [The Complete Works of Zhang Dainian]. 7 vols. Hong Kong: Man's Book Company, 1996.

Zhang Fuping. "Fuyu rensheng yi jiazhi he yiyi: yeshuo renwen jingshen" [Give Values and Significance to Human Life: Also on Humanism]. *Henan shehui kexue*, no. 5 (1999): 28–33.

Zhang Jinping. *Huwen yuannian: zhongguo de dierci zhuanxin* [The First Year of Hu and Wen in Power: the Second Transformation for China]. Taipei: Jieyou chubanshe, 2004.

Zhao, Yuezhi. "Falun Gong, Identity, and the Struggle over Meaning Inside and Outside China." In *Contesting Media Power: Alternative Media in a Networked World*, edited by Nick Couldry and James Curran, 209–23. Lanham, Md.: Rowman & Littlefield, 2003.

Zhao Yangong. "Hepin jiejue falun gong wenti" [Resolve the Issue of Falun Gong Peacefully]. *Beijing Spring* 83 (2000): 37–39.

Zheng, Yongnian. *Will China Become Democratic? Elite, Class, and Regime Transition.* Singapore: East Asian Institute, National University of Singapore, 2004.

Zheng Zhongyuan and Wang Yuqiang. 1976–1981 nian de zhongguo [China between 1976 and 1981]. Beijing: Zhongyang wenxian chubanshe, 1998.

"Zhi lianheguo mishuzhang annan de yifeng gongkaixin" [An Open Letter to UN Secretary General Annan]. *China Spring* 194 (1999): 63–64.

"Zhi quanguo renda daibiao de yifeng gong kaixin." [An Open Letter to the Delegates of the National People's Congress]. *China Spring* 194 (1999): 64–65.

"Zhonggong zhongyang guanyu falun gong de wenjian" [Documents of the Central Government on Falun Gong]. *Beijing Spring* 97 (2001): 9–12.

"Zhonggong zhongyang guanyu gongchandangyuan buzhun xiulian falun dafa de tongzhi" [The Central Committee Prohibits Communist Party Members from Practicing Falun Gong]. *People's Daily*, overseas edition, July 23, 1999.

"Zhongguo wangzhan mianlin dengji 'weiji'" [Chinese Internet Sites are Facing Peril]. Online at http://my.cnd.org/modules/wfsection/print.php?articleid=10458 (accessed June 27, 2005).

"Zhongguoren yali baogao: zhongchanjieceng bukan zhongfu" [Report on the Pressure the Chinese Feel: Middle Class Is Overwhelmed by Burden]. Online at http://my.cond.org/modules/wfsection/print.php?articleid=14593 (accessesd October 1, 2006).

Zhou, Xueguang. "Unorganized Interests and Collective Action in Communist China." *American Sociological Review* 58 (February 1993): 54–73.

Zhou, Yuqiong, and Patricia Moy. "Parsing Framing Process: The Interplay between Online Public Discourse and Media Coverage." *Journal of Communication* 57 (March 2007): 79–98.

Zhou Yousu. "Toushi yu shenjiu: Dui falun gong zhimizheng xianxiang de diaozha yu fenxi" [Reflection and Exploration: An Investigation and Analysis of the Phenomenon of Falun Gong Fanatics] *Shehui kexue fenxi*, no. 5 (2001): 104–9.

Zhu Xueqing. "Sixiangshi shang de shizongzhe" [The Person Lost in the History of Ideology]. In *1966: women nayidai de huiyi* [1966: Recollections of Our Generation], edited by Xu Youyu, 321–38. Beijing: Zhongguo wenlian chubanshe, 1998.